The Holiness and Honor of Praise

Also by Theda Holmes:
   How to Enjoy the Life of God
   Names of God Bible Studies I and II
   Hath God Said?

The Holiness and Honor of Praise

Theda Holmes
with Wendy Stackable and Kaye Moreno

Bridge Publishing, Inc.
Publishers of
LOGOS • HAVEN • OPEN SCROLL

All Scripture quotations are from the New American Standard Bible, © 1960, 1962, 1963, 1971, 1973, The Lockman Foundation. Used with permission.

References to Hebrew and Greek spellings and translations are from Strong's Exhaustive Concordance, MacDonald Publishing Co., MacLean, VA.

The Holiness and Honor of Praise
© 1986 Bridge Publishing, Inc.
All rights reserved.
Printed in the United States of America
ISBN 0-88270-599-7
Library of Congress catalog number 85-62801
Bridge Publishing, Inc.
2500 Hamilton Blvd.
South Plainfield, NJ 07080

This book is dedicated to
Jim, my precious husband,
and
Melinda, Mark, Mike,
and Sandi,
my children.

My greatest desire is that they
experience and share
the Holiness and Honor of Praise.

About the Author

Theda Holmes has spent fifteen years teaching praise and holiness in churches, conferences and retreats across the country. As well as having an extensive audio and video tape ministry and printed material available, she has been the guest on many Christian television and radio programs from coast to coast. Theda is also the director of Woman to Woman Ministries, Inc.

Table of Contents

Acknowledgments ix
Preface xi
Foreword xiii
Introduction xv

Part I
1 Entering the Land 3
2 Praise and Warfare in the Promised Land 15
3 Footholds of the Enemy 27

Part II
4 Captivity and Deliverance 33
5 Reasons for Praise: God's Worthiness 45
6 Other Reasons for Praise: 55
  Authority and Freedom
7 God's Picture of Worship: The Tabernacle 63
8 Entering Into Worship: The Priest 81
9 Anointed for Worship: The Oil 95
10 The Individual Life of Praise 103
11 Worshiping in Spirit and Truth 107
12 The Unity of the Faith: 117
   Worshiping With Other Believers
13 "You Shall Be My Witness": 129
   The Ministry of Reconciliation

Acknowledgments

I want to extend my gratitude to the following people for their help and contributions:

Wendy Stackable and Kaye Moreno,
two gifted writers who allowed the Lord of glory to fill their hearts and who served as scribes as God shared His message with us.

James and Betty Robison,
who have afforded me the privilege of serving the Lord with them for the past five years, and for the love and encouragement they've given.

J. Don George,
my pastor and friend whose support was constant as he encouraged me to be fulfilled in the gifts and callings of the Lord.

Jim, my husband.
Most of all I praise God for Jim, who has experienced with me all those ups and downs; he has seen me at my lowest ebb, and together we have experienced the mountaintop of God's glory, which makes the struggles worthwhile. I thank God for Jim's constant love and encouragement to find new ways of expressing God's greatness to others.

Preface

In 1970 I found myself to be a born-again Southern Baptist but spiritually dry. Most of my Christian life had been one of ups and downs that never brought true peace or stability for sustained periods of time. Like so many others, I too had tried to be an "overcomer," only to fail.

One Monday morning in March of 1970, alone in my bedroom I knelt by my bed and cried out to God, begging Him to come to my aid, to touch me, to love me—to do something. And he came! This Jesus who had seemed so vague, so historical, wrapped His loving arms around me and flooded my being with His holy light. I drank and drank it into myself. During that time we—Jesus and I—dealt with strongholds of sin and He set me on a spiritual journey that has been one joyous—and yet sometimes painful—learning experience after another.

The most obvious thing that was born that morning was a welling up of gratitude and great joy. I look back now and know it was the spirit of praise.

The Holiness and Honor of Praise

Fifteen years have passed since that life-changing day, and yet daily as I yield up myself to Him I am touched and changed even more.

This book is about people just like myself who needed God, who sought Him and found Him to be faithful. It is about the only One who can make our Christian life worth living—the author and initiator of praise. And it is filled with practical reasons and ways to praise the Lord and see His hand of deliverance move on our behalf. Praise is not only holy; it is an honor. It is a life to be lived. Join me in exalting His Name.

Theda Holmes

Foreword

I have known Theda Holmes as a friend and Christian co-worker for several years. She is a member of the church I pastor in Irving, Texas. It has been my delight to journey with the author of this book through the process of this manuscript's birth and ultimate completion.

I reviewed the manuscript in its embryonic stages; and now I have read it in its final form. I am pleased, as I know you will be, with what I have read.

Theda Holmes writes with clarity and conciseness. She communicates. You will not need to struggle to understand the concepts presented in this book. The Holy Spirit has beautifully packaged profound truth in an easy-to-understand format. Relax as you read and allow the revealed knowledge contained in this book to penetrate your spirit and probe your understanding.

Contained in this writing is a message so very relevant for these times. God has chosen to enthrone himself on the praises of His saints. Still, there is an additional message

The Holiness and Honor of Praise

which God desires to bring to you on these pages. Beyond the periphery of praise is a new dimension of His glory which all heaven desires to burst upon you.

Prepare to receive as you read. Get ready . . . be open to that precise Word that the Spirit will share with you. Make room in your mind, in your spirit, for something truly revelational. You will be glad you read this book.

J. Don George
Calvary Temple

Introduction

I will extol Thee, my God, O King;
And I will bless Thy name forever and ever.
Every day I will bless Thee,
And I will praise Thy name forever and ever.
Great is the Lord, and highly to be praised;
And His greatness is unsearchable.
One generation shall praise Thy works to another,
And shall declare Thy mighty acts.
On the glorious splendor of Thy majesty,
And on Thy wonderful works, I will meditate.
And men shall speak of the power of Thy awesome acts;
And I will tell of Thy greatness.
They shall eagerly utter the memory of Thine abundant goodness,
And shall shout joyfully of Thy righteousness.

Psalm 145:1-7

The Holiness and Honor of Praise

In late September, 1983, a well-known Bible teacher came into my office at the James Robison Evangelistic Association. He had just experienced a near fatal attack designed by the forces of evil to stop what God had planned for his future and for thousands who would hear the truth through him. On September 3, he had suffered a massive heart attack and stroke. His wife called several men and women, including James Robison, Jim Hylton and Dudley Hall, to rush to the home and pray.

This man was and is totally reliant on the Word of God. He had said many times that if he was going to teach the Bible he was surely going to live it. Even though many did not understand, the man refused medical treatment; instead, he began to quote the Word. For hours the atmosphere was filled with prayer, the Word of God, and praise. This concentration of God's power broke the power of Satan, and little by little the enemy had to release his deadly hold as life began to flow back into the man.

For days afterwards he rested in an atmosphere saturated with prayer, praise, and God's Word. Now, only a short time after his crisis, he was standing in my office giving testimony of the power of a mighty God. It was because of him that this book was born in my heart.

It is the unique privilege of God's people to magnify His holy name through praise. In praise we declare that God alone is supreme, able to meet every need by His righteousness. Through praise we are reminded of His constant love and the eternal covenant He established with all who call Him Lord.

Psalm 18:3 says, "I call upon the Lord, who is worthy to be praised, and I am saved from my enemies." Each of us is assaulted daily by the spiritual forces of darkness whose

Introduction

chief aim is to discredit the name of God and to destroy His people. Since Satan knows that praise asserts the very thing he is trying to destroy, he has gathered the enemies of praise to blind us to its significance. We find ourselves wondering, "What is the point of praise? Is it really that important?" It is, in fact, vital to our work with the Lord.

Praise affirms that God is our everything, completely sufficient to meet all our needs. Psalm 145:14-16 says, "The Lord sustains all who fall, and raises up all who are bowed down. The eyes of all look to Thee, and Thou dost give them their food in due time. Thou dost open Thy hand, and dost satisfy the desire of every living thing."

Praise also reminds us that the Lord is faithful to His covenant people. While Psalms 105, 106 and 107 describe the unfaithfulness of Israel, they also point out God's merciful deliverance because of the covenant He had made with Abraham, Isaac, and Jacob. Psalm 89:1 declares, "I will sing of the lovingkindness of the Lord forever; to all generations I will make known Thy faithfulness with my mouth."

Praise announces our position in Christ and recognizes His authority over the enemy. Psalm 138:7-8 says, "Though I walk in the midst of trouble, Thou wilt revive me; Thou wilt stretch forth Thy hand against the wrath of my enemies, and Thy right hand will save me. The Lord will accomplish what concerns me; Thy lovingkindness, O Lord, is everlasting; do not forsake the works of Thy hands."

Finally, praise causes us to search our own souls in light of God's holiness as it draws us nearer to Him. Psalm 139 is a clear picture of this:

The Holiness and Honor of Praise

O Lord, Thou hast searched me and known me.
Thou dost know when I sit down and when I rise up;
Thou dost understand my thought from afar.
Thou dost scrutinize my path and my lying down,
And art intimately acquainted with all my ways. . . .
How precious also are Thy thoughts to me, O God!
How vast is the sum of them!
If I should count them, they would outnumber the sand.
When I awake, I am still with Thee. . . .
Search me, O God, and know my heart;
Try me and know my anxious thoughts;
And see if there be any hurtful way in me,
And lead me in the everlasting way.

(verses 1-3, 17, 18, 23, 24)

A Covenant Worthy of Praise

God has established an eternal covenant with us, and it is important that we understand its meaning in light of the Scriptures. A covenant is a sacred act in which two individuals become one. The closest picture we have of this in our culture today is marriage. A person in true covenant dare not break it without serious consequences resulting.

Everything God does in our lives is based on covenant. Through it we die to self in order to take on His life. Without it, we are trapped in our sin. In the Old Testament, a covenant was formalized through at least six different steps. First, the two people exchanged robes, signifying the exchange of their identities. Both Joseph and the prodigal son received their father's fine robes in exchange for the filthy garments they wore (see Genesis 37:2-3; Luke 15:11-24).

Introduction

Second, they would exchange belts, which represented their strength. They also exchanged weapons, meaning they would take on the other person's enemies as their own. David and Jonathan followed these steps when they pledged themselves to one another in 1 Samuel 18:1-4.

Next, an animal would be split from top to bottom, and the two people would take a "walk of blood" through the cut pieces, meeting in the middle and saying, "You do this to me and more if I break our covenant." When God established His covenant with Abram in Genesis 15:7-21, He alone passed through the pieces, since only He was able to keep the covenant entirely.

After the "walk of blood," the people exchanged names. Abram became Abraham, and Jehovah became the God of Abraham.

Finally, the two people would eat from the same bread and drink from the same cup, testifying to all of their commitment to one another. Thereafter, they would be known as friends.

Likewise, God has given us the identity and strength of Jesus, and we have accepted His enemies as our own. To demonstrate the seriousness of His commitment to the Father on our behalf, Jesus took a "walk of blood," becoming both sacrifice and high priest (Hebrews 9:11-12). He humbled himself and was called the Son of Man; we, on the other hand, are called Christians, or "little Christs," the children of God (Philippians 2:5-8; Acts 11:26). We have also partaken of the communion bread and wine, representing Jesus' body and blood, to declare our supernatural partnership with the Lord (1 Corinthians 11:23-28).

Such a covenant is indeed worthy of praise, and it is our great privilege to explore it more fully through God's Word.

Part I

Chapter 1
Entering the Land

To experience the birth of a child can be a blessed event for a man and woman in love. Likewise, the second birth is a blessed event for the man or woman who in love turns to Jesus for salvation. In the life of every growing Christian there is another birth experience, the birth of praise to Almighty God.

This study focuses on the tribe of Judah in particular, which in Hebrew means "praise." For Christians, who are the spiritual Israel according to Romans 9:6-8 and Galatians 3:7-9, there is a fundamental truth presented in Genesis 35: *Praise is the fruit of a life lived at the altar of God.* In verse 1 God spoke to Jacob (Israel) and instructed him to "arise, go up to Bethel, and *live* there; and make an altar there to God, who appeared to you when you fled from your brother Esau."

So Jacob told his household and the others with him, "Put away the foreign gods which are among you, and purify yourselves, and change your garments; and let us

The Holiness and Honor of Praise

arise and go up to Bethel; and I will make an altar there to God, who answered me in the day of my distress, and has been with me wherever I have gone" (verses 2, 3).

It is interesting that certain things happened before they left for their journey to build God's altar. First, Jacob instructed them to put away all idols among them. It was not a question of whether or not idols were present; he knew they were.

Ezekiel 14:3 says men "set up their idols in their hearts," and Colossians 3:5 tells us specifically what constitutes idols in our lives today:

> Therefore consider the members of your earthly body as dead to immorality, impurity, passion, evil desire, and greed, which amounts to idolatry.

All of us worships something or someone, but the critical question is, "Who or what is the object of our worship?" In order to build an altar that will be acceptable to God, all idolatry must be dealt with.

Second, Jacob told his people to purify themselves. This purification came through ceremonial washings, which were later instituted in Leviticus 8:7. Today, our cleansing comes through the purifying fire of God's Holy Spirit (Matthew 3:11-12) and the washing of water by the living Word (Ephesians 5:26). Jesus prayed that we would be made holy when He prayed in John 17:17, "Sanctify them in the truth; Thy Word is truth."

Third, Jacob told the people to change their garments. In modern language he was saying something like this: "Tomorrow we are going to take a trip to worship Holy God. I want you to do three things: rid yourselves of

Entering the Land

any object that might take preeminence over God and would displease Him, take a bath and change your clothes."

We are taking a spiritual trip. We are going home, and our garments must not only be clean, but designed and provided by God alone.

In his book, *The Study of the Types*,* Ada R. Habershon sheds further light on the garments we are to wear: "Man is often inclined to try to patch up the old rags and put on 'some of self and some of Thee'; but Christ's parable tells us how useless this is."

> But no one puts a patch of unshrunk cloth on an old garment; for the patch pulls away from the garment, and a worse tear results. Nor do men put new wine into old wineskins; otherwise, the wineskins burst, and wine pours out, and the wineskins are ruined; but they put new wine into fresh wineskins, and both are preserved.
>
> Matthew 9:16-17

Ecclesiastes 9:8a says, "Let your clothes be white [i.e., holy] all the time." James added that they should be "unstained by the world" (James 1:27). Isaiah 61:10 proclaims, "I will rejoice greatly in the Lord, my soul will exult in my God; for He has clothed me with garments of salvation, He has wrapped me with a robe of righteousness; as a bridegroom decks himself with a garland, and as a bride adorns herself with her jewels." According

---

* Ada R. Habershon, *The Study of the Types*, (Grand Rapids, MI: 1975).

The Holiness and Honor of Praise

to Isaiah 61:3, praise, salvation and righteousness are the garments of holiness we are to put on if we wish to come to the altar of God.

In Genesis 35:5-7 we read that "as they journeyed, there was *a great terror upon the cities which were around them,* and they did not pursue the sons of Jacob. So Jacob came to . . . Bethel, which is in the land of Caanan, he and all the people who were with him" (italics added). Another name for Bethel is Luz, which means "fruitfulness." The root word is related to the almond, a particular fruit that is "born" early and remains firm. "And he built an altar there, and called the place El-bethel, because there God had revealed Himself to him, when he fled from his brother" (verse 7). Jacob was obedient and as a result, God protected him, and all the surrounding tribes experienced the awesome fear of God.

God wants to bring us to the spiritual Canaan, the land of abundant life, as found in John 10:10. He wants our spiritual "house" to be fruitful and for that fruit to remain. Just as Jacob and his household worshiped God at the altar in Bethel, we are to dwell at the altar of God, presenting ourselves as living sacrifices to the Lord (Romans 12:1-2). "And coming to Him as to a living stone, rejected by men, but choice and precious in the sight of God, you also, as living stones, are being built up as a spiritual house for a holy priesthood, to offer up spiritual sacrifices acceptable to God through Jesus Christ" (1 Peter 2:4-5).

Thus, it is our privilege and responsibility to live in praise and service to the Lord. Then, when we have been established at the altar we will begin to see new life that will ultimately point people to Christ.

Entering the Land

Jacob had twelve sons who became leaders of the tribes of Israel (Genesis 29:32-35; 30:1-25; and 35:16-18). Through the prompting of the Holy Spirit, each son was given a name that carries a special meaning, relevant for us today:

1. Reuben: "See, a son!"
2. Simeon: "Hearing"
3. Levi: "Attached, intwined"
4. Judah: "Praise"
5. Issachar: "Reward"
6. Zebulun: "Habitation, dwell with"
7. Joseph: "Adding to"
8. Benjamin: "Son of the right hand"
9. Dan: "Judge"
10. Naphtali: "My wrestling"
11. Gad: "Deity, fortune"
12. Asher: "Happy"

God could have chosen to send Jesus through the tribe of spiritual wrestling, or through rewards, or happiness, or judgment, or any of the others, but He chose to send His only Son through Judah, which means "praise."

Deuteronomy 10:21a tells us, "He is your praise and He is your God. . . ." It is indeed through a life of praise that Jesus is manifested to the world.

We must understand that *praise is not simply an emotional outburst but rather a lifestyle.* We must walk confidently into the power of praise if we expect to see the mighty hand of God on our behalf.

God commanded His people to praise Him and declared that it was "becoming to the upright." In other words, we look good praising God, and He takes pleasure in it.

The Holiness and Honor of Praise

> You who fear the Lord, praise Him; all you descendants of Jacob, glorify Him, and stand in awe of Him, all you descendants of Israel.
>
> Psalm 22:23

> Sing for joy in the Lord, O you righteous ones; praise is becoming to the upright.
>
> Psalm 33:1

> Praise the Lord, all nations; laud Him, all peoples!
>
> Psalm 117:1

God is enthroned on praise, and it is our declaration of His majesty which brings Him on the scene in our lives.

> Yet Thou art holy, O Thou who art enthroned upon the praises of Israel.
>
> Psalm 22:3

> Who is like Thee, majestic in holiness, awesome in praises, working wonders?
>
> Exodus 15:11

God has given us a joyful responsibility to proclaim His righteousness with our lips, hands and through music. This is to be a part of our life style. In the Old Testament there are eight different Hebrew words which indicate the various expressions of praise and the progression towards true worship.

1. Towdah

Praise begins as an act of our will. *Towdah* means "the extension of the hand: a sacrifice of praise and thanksgiving, by a choir of worshipers." This word is used in the following Scriptures:

Entering the Land

> With the voice of joy and thanksgiving (praise), a multitude keeping festival.
>
> Psalm 42:4c

> He who offers a sacrifice of thanksgiving (praise) honors Me; and to him who orders his way aright I shall show the salvation of God.
>
> Psalm 50:23

2. Yadah

Praise then develops into a desire. I want to praise the Lord. *Yadah* means "the extended or lifted arm with hands open and upward." This signifies our surrender to God's power, His direction and abilities. It is accompanied with the giving of thanks and confession of the Lord's greatness. *Yadah* is the word used in the following verses:

> I will give thanks to the Lord according to His righteousness, and will sing praises to the name of the Lord Most High.
>
> Psalm 7:17

> Let the peoples praise Thee, O God; Let all the peoples praise Thee.
>
> Psalm 67:3

3. Shabach

As we enter into a deeper awareness of God through an act of our will which becomes the desire of our heart, our immediate response is to begin giving God glory. *Shabach* means "to address with a loud voice, to pacify with words; commend, give glory." This is the word used in the following Scriptures:

The Holiness and Honor of Praise

> Because Thy lovingkindness is better than life, my lips will praise thee.
>
> Psalm 63:3

> Praise the Lord, all nations; laud Him, all peoples!
>
> Psalm 117:1

> One generation shall praise Thy works to another, and shall declare Thy mighty acts.
>
> Psalm 145:4

4. Halal

This word means "to make a show, to boast, shine, brag upon, to look foolish." At this point of praise we have ceased to be self-conscious and are totally caught up in magnifying the wonders of the Lord. This kind of praise might look foolish to men, but to an all-wise God, praise is never foolishness; He loves it. In fact, He loves it so much that He will prove himself mighty on behalf of those who would dare to look foolish in the eyes of man as they boast in their God. This is the word used in the following Scriptures:

> And they are to stand every morning to thank and to praise the Lord, and likewise at evening.
>
> 1 Chronicles 23:30

> So they sang praises with joy, and bowed down and worshiped.
>
> 2 Chronicles 29:30b

5. Zamar

This word means "to touch the strings of an instrument, accompanied by the voice; to sing psalms." This is the extent of all we can do physically to show our praise to the Lord. It is used in the following Scripture:

> My heart is steadfast, O God, my heart is steadfast; I will sing, yes, I will sing praises! Awake, my glory; awake, harp and lyre, I will awaken the dawn!
>
> Psalm 57:7-8

6. Bawrak

Bawrak means to "bless God, to kneel down in expectancy." After our expressions of extended arms upward to Him and our loud words of praise, we begin to move into His holy presence. *Bawrak* speaks of the transition from praise to worship and is used in the following Scripture:

> And let them pray [invoke His ear] for him continually; let them bless Him all day long.
>
> Psalm 72:15

7. Tehillah

God's throne, His holy habitation rests upon *tehillah*. Its meaning is "laudation or hymn." At this point, praise ceases to be an outward expression and becomes a way of life, for it is abiding in the presence of God that changes our lives.

> He is your praise and He is your God, who has done these great and awesome things for you which your eyes have seen.
>
> Deuteronomy 10:21

The Holiness and Honor of Praise

> Arise, bless the Lord your God forever and ever!
>
> Nehemiah 9:5b
>
> Yet Thou art holy, O Thou who art enthroned upon the praises of Israel.
>
> Psalm 22:3

8. Hilluwl

This word means "rejoicing, a celebration of thanksgiving for the harvest, to be merry." It is used only once in the Scriptures.

> But in the fourth year all its fruits shall be holy, an offering of praise to the Lord.
>
> Leviticus 19:24

Certainly all these expressions of praise have a legitimate place in the Christian's life. What an honor it is to extend our arms upward, and in doing so, tell God we know He is all-powerful and full of authority, and that we gladly submit to Him. What a joy to boast in our God, to tell about His wonders and His grace. How great to celebrate His presence with shouts, songs, musical instruments, and the dance—and to kneel down in holy adoration before Him.

Praise is a tremendous privilege, and the more we understand its importance and the enemy's assaults on it, the freer we will be to honor the Lord with a life of praise.

> From the rising of the sun to its setting the name of the Lord is to be praised (*halal*). Praise the Lord! Praise, O servants of the Lord.

Entering the Land

Praise the name of the Lord. Blessed be the name of the Lord from this time forth and forever.

Psalm 113:3, 1-2

Chapter 2
Praise and Warfare in the Promised Land

The book of Joshua records the Israelites' occupation of Canaan. It was here that God wanted to demonstrate His might and faithfulness once again. After the death of Moses, God assured Joshua "Just as I have been with Moses, I will be with you; I will not fail you or forsake you" (Joshua 1:5). Thus, it was a strong, courageous Joshua who led the people into the promised land.

From the beginning he instructed the Israelites, "Consecrate yourselves, for tomorrow the Lord will do wonders among you" (3:5). He told the priests, "Take up the ark of the covenant and cross over ahead of the people" (verse 6).

God had promised to give His people and their descendants the promised land, but they had to be dedicated to His worship and obedient to His law. In return for their faithfulness, the Lord worked with them to dispossess the pagans from the land (Joshua 3:10).

The Holiness and Honor of Praise

The root meanings of each of the tribal names found in Joshua 3 are significant:

1. "Canaanite" comes from the root meaning "to press down," and implies depression
2. "Hittite" comes from "fear, terror"
3. "Hivite" comes from "compromise"
4. "Perizzite" comes from "lack of commitment"
5. "Girgashite" comes from "strangers"
6. "Amorite" comes from "words or murmurings"
7. "Jebusite" comes from "heaviness'

We struggle with these same spiritual enemies today as we strive to possess our own inheritance in Jesus. The contemporary church is filled with depression, fear, compromise, lack of commitment, strangers, words and heaviness. God wants to bring deliverance, but we must be prepared to fight spiritual battles if these enemies are to be defeated in our lives.

The Enemies of Praise

In 2 Chronicles 20 the sons of Moab, the sons of Ammon and the sons of Mount Seir joined forces against Judah to destroy God's people of praise.

Verse 2 says, "A great multitude is coming against you from beyond the sea, out of Syria (or Aram), and behold, they are in Hazazon-tamar (that is, En-gedi)."

Aram is Hebrew for "high places or lands." These high places generally were locations of worship, particularly Baal worship. Ephesians 6:12 says, "For our struggle is not against flesh and blood, but against the rulers, against the powers, against the world forces of this darkness, against the spiritual forces of wickedness in the heavenly places."

Praise and Warfare in the Promised Land

Hazazon-tamar means "division." The children of Moab, Ammon and Mount Seir were motivated by the "spiritual wickedness in high places," even though they were three adversaries, independent of one another.

Unlike the seven tribes Joshua fought earlier when the people first crossed over into the promised land, these three tribes had been given access to the territory. In God's strength, Joshua led the Israelites to victory, but Moab, Ammon and Mount Seir had to be dealt with by God alone. This was accomplished later, during the reign of Jehoshaphat, who was a king of Judah who attempted to be obedient to God. When he saw the trouble his people were in—and the impossibility of human victory—he responded in several ways:

1. He was afraid
2. He turned his attention to seek the Lord
3. He proclaimed a fast throughout all Judah
4. He brought the people of praise together
5. They all called out to God as a unit.

As a result, the people throughout the land saw the awesome power and sovereignty of God.

Biblical history tells us clearly who these terrible enemies were:

1. *The sons of Ammon.* These are the descendants of the "incestuous son of Lot," and their name carries with it a sense of depravity. They were also called Zamzumites in Deuteronomy 2:19, 20, 37, a name which means "to plan, consider, devise, imagine, plot, purpose, think evil." The sons of Ammon were a threat to Israel on several occasions. They encouraged marriages between themselves and God's people and led Israel into idol worship. Their

The Holiness and Honor of Praise

abominations continued to affect the Israelites in the time of Ezra (see Ezra 9:1) and Nehemiah (see Nehemiah 2:10, 19; 4:3, 7; 13:1, 23). In Zephaniah 2:8-11 they were threatened with total destruction because they reviled Judah and magnified themselves against Jehovah.

These people represent the world and the degenerate man whose conscience has been seared because of sin. Romans 1:25, 28 describes the reprobate mind:

> For they exchanged the truth of God for a lie, and worshiped and served the creature rather than the Creator, who is blessed forever. . . . And just as they did not see fit to acknowledge God any longer, God gave them over to a depraved mind, to do those things which are not proper.

Second Timothy 3:8, 9 explains further:

> And just as Jannes and Jambres opposed Moses, so these men also oppose the truth, men of depraved mind, rejected as regards the faith. But they will not make further progress; for their folly will be obvious to all, as also that of those two came to be.

2. *The sons of Moab*. *Moab* is a Hebrew word meaning "tribal, congregated unit, flock, folks." Historically, Moab was another incestuous son of Lot, but the emphasis here is different than with the sons of Ammon.

As a tribe, they were frequently aligned with Ammon to fight Israel and draw them away from God (see Judges 3:13; Nehemiah 13:1, 2, 23 and Psalm 83). As a spiritual enemy of the people of praise, they could represent those

Praise and Warfare in the Promised Land

---

closest to us whose hearts war against Almighty God. They may be family members, friends, members of the church—the ones we love but who are not wholly dedicated to the Lord.

David, another king of Judah (praise), said in Psalm 55:12-14:

> For it is not an enemy who reproaches me, then I could bear it; nor is it one who hates me who has exalted himself against me, then I could hide myself from him. But it is you, a man my equal, my companion and my familiar friend. We who had sweet fellowship together, walked in the house of God in the throng.

In Psalm 41:9 he says,

> Even my closest friend in whom I trusted, who ate my bread, has lifted up his heel against me.

3. *The sons of Mount Seir.* The Hebrew word for "mount" in this context means "obstacle," and "Seir" means "shaggy goat, devil, satyr." The dictionary defines a satyr as "any of a class of minor woodland deities, attendant on Bacchus, usually represented as having pointed ears, short horns, the head and body of a man, and the legs of a goat, and as being fond of riotous merriment and lechery (i.e., an insatiable sexual desire); a lustful or lecherous man."

Specific reference to satyrs is made in 2 Chronicles 11:15 when Jereboam rebelled against the Lord: "And he set up priests of his own for the high places, for the satyrs, and for the calves which he had made."

The Holiness and Honor of Praise

The sons of Mount Seir are the descendants of Esau, who sold his inheritance to gratify a physical need (Genesis 25:29-34). Esau is a type of the flesh-nature which always chooses to indulge itself at the expense of godliness.

Historically, Esau's descendants also gave up their spiritual inheritance to follow false gods. In essence, they pledged themselves, perhaps unknowingly, to the chief enemy of praise, Satan, who is frequently represented in drawings and paintings as a goat or goat-man.

There are indications in Isaiah 14:11 and Ezekiel 28:13-15 that Lucifer was the leader of praise before he was thrown out of heaven. After his expulsion, Satan's ultimate goal was to strike back at God. Thus, he decided to pollute God's chosen people, who had been created to serve and praise the Lord. The church is pictured throughout the Bible as the Bride of Christ, and so Satan has set out to make this Bride spiritually adulterous by getting her into bed with the world through compromise and intimidation. The children of Mount Seir are historical types who show something of the dark works of the devil.

Victory Through Praise

Praise instantly brings God into any situation to win the battle men cannot fight. God wants to bring the spirit of praise back to His people today so they might "stand and see the salvation of the Lord."

God has judged the enemies of praise to be the spiritual counterparts to the sons of Moab, Ammon and Mount Seir. Let's review the significance this has for us:

Praise and Warfare in the Promised Land

---

1. *The sons of Moab.* The root meaning of Moab means "tribal, congregated unit, flock, folks" and might apply to family, friends or church members who are not committed to the Lord. Jeremiah 48:7 declares, "For because of your trust in your own achievements and treasures, even you yourself will be captured; and Chemosh (their god to whom Solomon built an altar to honor "power") will go off into exile together with his priests and his princes."

2. *The sons of Ammon.* The root meaning of Ammon implies depravity. Ammon was one of the incestuous sons of Lot. These are the reprobates who have rejected God and given themselves over to the ways of the world. Jeremiah 49:2, 3 says, " 'Therefore behold, the days are coming,' declares the Lord, 'That I shall cause a trumpet blast of war to be heard against Rabbah (meaning "abundance") of the sons of Ammon; and it will become a desolate heap, and her towns will be set on fire. Then Israel will take possession of his possessors,' says the Lord. . . . For Malcom (meaning "status, royalty") will go off into exile together with his priests and his princes" (NASB).

3. *The sons of Mount Seir.* Mount means "obstacle," and Seir means "devil, satyr," a picture of Satan, the great seducer of the Church. Ezekiel 35:1-6 pronounces, "Moreover, the word of the Lord came to me saying, 'Son of man, set your face against Mount Seir, and prophesy against it, and say to it, "Thus says the Lord God, Behold *I* am against you, Mount Seir, and *I* will stretch out *My* hand against you, and *I* will make you a desolation and a waste. *I* will lay waste your cities, and you will become a

The Holiness and Honor of Praise

desolation. Then you will know that *I am the Lord*. Because you have had *everlasting enmity* [see Genesis 3:15] and have delivered the sons of Israel to the power of the sword at the time of their calamity, at the time of the punishment of the end, therefore, as I live," declares the Lord God, "*I* will give you over to bloodshed, and bloodshed will pursue you; since you have not hated bloodshed, therefore bloodshed will pursue you" ' " (italics added).

Praise God for the Cross of Jesus Christ! It is His shed blood which is held up against the enemies of praise today. His blood pursues and overtakes all the works of darkness. Through Jesus' blood alone we stand to praise and magnify the matchless name of the Lord our God.

> Now the salvation, and the power, and the kingdom of our God and the authority of His Christ have come, for the accuser of our brethren has been thrown down, who accuses them before our God day and night. And they overcame him because of the blood of the Lamb and because of the word of their testimony [praise], and they did not love their life even to death.
> Revelation 12:11

God's Battle
Through praise, God delivered the Israelites. Second Chronicles 20:21 says, "When he [Jehoshaphat] had consulted with the people, he appointed those who sang to the Lord and those who praised Him in holy attire, as they went out before the army and said, 'Give thanks to the Lord, for His lovingkindness is everlasting.' "

Praise and Warfare in the Promised Land

The Hebrew word for "praise" in this verse is *yadah*, which means "to extend your arms upward with palms open, signifying God's power and authority." This kind of praise is accompanied by confessions of the Lord's eternal goodness and love.

Those who praised God here did so in holy attire. Likewise, we never come to God clothed in anything less than the righteousness of Jesus, borne out in our lives every day. Second Corinthians 5:21 says, "He made Him who knew no sin to be sin on our behalf that we might become the righteousness of God in Him." Words of praise without a life of praise are meaningless, but glorifying words coupled with a life of holiness both bless and please God—and defeat the enemy. Psalm 50:23 says:

> He who offers a sacrifice of thanksgiving honors Me; and to him who orders his way aright I shall show the salvation of God.

In this setting, "The Lord set ambushes against the sons of Ammon, Moab and Mount Seir, who had come up against Judah; so they were routed. For the sons of Ammon and Moab rose up against the inhabitants of Mount Seir destroying them completely, and when they had finished with the inhabitants of Seir, they helped to destroy one another" (2 Chronicles 20:22-23).

Wandering Eyes and a Wandering Heart

In the height of victory Jehoshaphat and his people claimed a vast wealth of goods as spoil from the battle, including beautiful garments. They were three days gathering everything together because there was so much.

The Holiness and Honor of Praise

On the fourth day, they assembled at a place called Beracah, which means "blessing" in Hebrew. Second Chronicles 20:27 says they returned home "with joy, for the Lord had made them to rejoice over their enemies." It was a magnificent sight, to be sure—a small band of Israelites carrying off the rewards of a battle God had won for them. Verse 30 says the dread of God fell on all the surrounding kingdoms as a result, and the Lord gave Israel rest on all sides.

But this chapter ends with a warning. The high places built to honor false gods were not removed, and the people did not turn their hearts toward God completely (1 Kings 22:43).

In the midst of excitement and content, Jehoshaphat himself forgot the counsel of the Lord and made an unholy alliance with the king of Israel, Ahaziah, who followed Baal and thus provoked God. The alliance they made was primarily a business venture in which they planned to build ships to go down to Tarshish, which means "pleasantness" in Hebrew. However, God brought judgment down upon Jehoshaphat's plan and destroyed the ships.

As God's people, we are to seek His direction in every decision. Temptation often follows close behind victory, and so it is imperative that we be listening for the Lord's voice. We are called to be holy, set apart for God's purposes (see Deuteronomy 7:6 and 1 Peter 2:9). We are commanded not to be unequally yoked to the world, regardless of how harmless a joint effort of some kind may seem. Second Corinthians 6:14 says:

Praise and Warfare in the Promised Land

Do not be bound together with unbelievers; for what partnership have righteousness and lawlessness, or what fellowship has light with darkness?

We are to be pure, fixing our eyes not on earthly treasures, but on those laid up in heaven, "for where your treasure is, there will your heart be also" (Matthew 6:19-21).

Chapter 3
Footholds of the Enemy

We can trace the foothold which the sons of Ammon, Moab and Mount Seir had in Canaan back to King Solomon. Prior to his reign, Israel was united; yet, because of Solomon's unfaithfulness to the Lord, all the tribes except Judah were taken away from him. God left Judah because of His covenant with David; He had promised to raise up the Messiah out of David's lineage (see 1 Kings 11:12, 13).

Solomon was the son of David, the great king of praise. With his reign the decline of a people created to worship God began by his own perpetuation of heathen altars.

Although he is considered to be the wisest man who ever lived, Solomon may have become the greatest fool. He had seven hundred wives and three hundred concubines, most of whom were idolaters and daughters of pagan princes (see 1 Kings 11:1-8). Solomon built altars for them on the Mount of Olives, east of Jerusalem where he built the temple to Jehovah (verse 7). It should be noted that among

The Holiness and Honor of Praise

these heathen wives were women from the tribes of Ammon, Moab and Edom (or Mount Seir).

Verses 4-8 say that Solomon's heart went after three gods in particular:

1. Ashtoreth (verse 5), which indicates increase. The Hebrew root means "to accumulate, to grow rich."
2. Milcom (verse 5), the god of the Ammonites (see 2 Chronicles 20:10). The Hebrew root means "royalty, status."
3. Chemosh (verse 7), "the detestable idol of Moab" (see 2 Chronicles 20:10). The Hebrew root describes power and means specifically "to subdue."

Solomon committed spiritual adultery, giving the devil a foothold in God's territory. As a result, a mighty kingdom was divided. The sins of the fathers were indeed passed on to the children to the third and fourth generation (Exodus 20:5).

Power, status, and wealth captured the heart of a man originally committed to God. In 2 Chronicles 20:25-33 these same enticements captured the people's hearts, even after great victory. Today power, status, and wealth are respected and, in some circles, revered. Men and women place a high premium on fleshly gain, often at the expense of true heavenly reward.

Solomon built altars to gods which represented success. He built places of worship on high places throughout the kingdom. It is important for us to understand why places of false worship must be torn down and why allegiance must be paid to God alone.

Footholds of the Enemy

The Hebrew for "high places" here is *bamah*, which means "heights of Baal." Sacrifices were made to the collective gods known as Baal on these high places. The root word for "Baal" means "to be master of, to marry and have dominion over, to be the husband of." Though Jesus is the Bridegroom of the Church, this is a position Satan has always wanted for himself. He is an imitator of truth and a spoiler of all that is holy.

Our hearts must be turned continually toward the Lord if we are to be people of His covenant. Isaiah 57:15 says it is God who dwells on the high and holy place. We must be aware that Satan, who tried to usurp God's throne in heaven, will also try to counterfeit that high and holy place within our hearts.

Part II

Chapter 4
Captivity and Deliverance

For hundreds of years Judah lived in and out of captivity. The bondage she experienced under each nation was designed by Satan to bring a specific affliction upon God's people of praise.

Egypt: "beseige and distress"

Egypt was the land of Ham (Psalm 105:23; 106:22), a fertile area that prospered in many ways. The Pharaohs who reigned sought counsel from magis, priests, and idols. When Moses went to Egypt to seek the release of the Israelites, he was met with great indignation. God's people were treated as little more than possessions. Because of the Egyptians' unwillingness to yield to God, they suffered terrible famine and various plagues. Their army was eventually drowned in the Red Sea, but the Jews passed over on dry land, and were safely delivered out of their hands.

The Holiness and Honor of Praise

> Thou art my hiding place; Thou dost preserve me from trouble; Thou dost surround me with songs of deliverance.
> Psalm 32:7

> Then they cried out to the Lord in their trouble; He delivered them out of their distresses.
> Psalm 107:6

Egypt here represents the *world* and all its trappings. The person who clamors after the things of the world will indeed be beseiged by it and fall into distress. Only in God do we find our needs met completely.

Assyria: "going straight towards prosperity"

The nation of Assyria was founded by Nimrod, as recorded in Genesis 10:8-12. It was a primary seat of commerce and productivity. The people of Assyria worshiped four gods in particular—Adrammelech, Anammelech, Nisroch and Tartak.

Assyria may symbolize the *flesh*, which constantly seeks to satisfy its own desires. Here no room is made for servanthood and charity, only greed. Yet, God's very nature is a giving one. He gave His only Son so we could find life, and He will surely not hold back those other things we need to grow and be conformed to Him.

> The Lord is my shepherd, I shall not want.
> Psalm 23:1

> O taste and see that the Lord is good; how blessed is the man who takes refuge in Him!

Captivity and Deliverance

> O fear the Lord, you His saints; for to those who fear Him, there is no want.
>
> Psalm 34:8-9

Babylon: "confusion"

Babylon was also built by Nimrod and is called the land of Shinar in Genesis 10:10; 11:2; 14:1, 9. It is also referred to as the land of Sheshach in Jeremiah 25 and the land of Meratham in Jeremiah 50. The government of Babylon was a limited monarchy noted for its tyranny.

Babylon may be a type for the *devil,* who is the author of all confusion. We find ourselves often bombarded by a myriad of thoughts, all racing about in our heads, deterring us from doing God's will. First Corinthians 14:33 says "God is not a God of confusion but of peace," and we may rest in that fact. His grace alone will enable us to carry out His Word at the proper time and in the proper manner.

> Why are you in despair, O my soul? And why have you become disturbed within me? Hope in God, for I shall again praise Him for the help of His presence.
>
> Psalm 42:5

> Surely I have composed and quieted my soul; like a weaned child rests against his mother, my soul is like a weaned child within me. O Israel, hope in the Lord from this time forth and forever.
>
> Psalm 131:2-3

Media-Persia: "to be brought low, to pierce with iron"

Scripture refers to Media as a powerful country, which placed great emphasis on its binding laws. Persia, on the other hand, was founded by Cyrus and dominated Asia from 539 to 331 B.C. Bound by the Tigris River on the west and south, the Inders Valley on the east, and the Armenian Ranges and Caspian Sea on the north, Persia covered one million square miles.

The Media-Persian Empire might represent the *lust of the flesh,* referred to in 1 John 2:16. The flesh never stops wanting to be satisfied, and if we try to fulfill the desires of the flesh, we will be dominated by an increasingly binding force. Even our spiritual efforts will turn sour as we become tied to laws and tradition. It is only through the finished work at Calvary that we will find true freedom and fulfillment.

> He brought me up out of the pit of destruction, out of the miry clay; and He set my feet upon a rock making my footsteps firm. And He put a new song in my mouth, a song of praise to our God; many will see and fear, and will trust in the Lord.
>
> Psalm 40:2-3

> Let the high praises of God be in their mouth, and a two-edged sword in their hand, to execute vengeance on the nations, and punishment on the peoples; to bind their kings with chains, and their nobles with fetters of iron.
>
> Psalm 149:6-8

Captivity and Deliverance

Greece: "to effervesce like a hot, intoxicating liquid"

Greece was an area of major cultural importance for many years. Its orderly system of life was based on knowledge and art and is responsible for many of our modern definitions of truth and beauty.

Greece might well typify the *lust of the eyes* which makes us drunk on the things of the world. It is always dangerous to focus our eyes on blessings rather than the Blesser. Second Corinthians 4:18 says we are to "look not at the things which are seen, but at the things which are not seen; for the things which are seen are temporal, but the things which are not seen are eternal." Beauty and Truth are found in Jesus, and unless we direct our search in Him alone, we will become blind to the life God has given us to enjoy in Him.

> As the deer pants for the water brooks, so my soul pants for Thee, O God. My soul thirsts for God, for the living God.
>
> Psalm 42:1-2
>
> He causes the grass to grow for the cattle, and vegetation for the labor of man, so that he may bring forth food from the earth, and wine which makes man's heart glad, so that he may make his face glisten with oil, and food which sustains man's heart.
>
> Psalm 104:14-15

Rome: "strength"

The Roman Empire was well known for its advanced roadways and water systems, its highly developed laws, its courts, and its adventurous myths. It was a progressive

The Holiness and Honor of Praise

country, founded in 753 B.C. A monarchy until 509 B.C., Rome was a republic from 509 until 31 B.C. when it became an empire that embraced all Italy and the Mediterranean world, half of Britain, the Rhine and Danube Rivers and as far as Parthia. Moral corruption led to its decline and fall in the fifth century. Unfortunately, America today has been compared to Rome.

Because of its rapid progress, Rome was hailed for its achievements and thereby grew proud and powerful. Herein is the *boastful pride of life* we are warned against in 1 John 2:16. When pride becomes the stimulus to achieve, we become trapped and our vision is clouded. It is God who grants success (Proverbs 8:12-21; 10:22). We must learn to glory in our weakness that the strength of God might rest upon us. As 2 Corinthians 12:9-10 says, "And He has said to me, 'My grace is sufficient for you, for power is perfected in weakness.' Most gladly, therefore, I will rather boast about my weaknesses, that the power of Christ may dwell in me. Therefore I am well content with weaknesses, with insults, with distresses, with persecutions, with difficulties, for Christ's sake; for when I am weak, then I am strong."

> God is our refuge and strength, a very present help in trouble.
>
> Psalm 46:1
>
> O my strength, I will sing praises to Thee; for God is my stronghold, the God who shows me lovingkindness.
>
> Psalm 59:17

Captivity and Deliverance

Out of Dry Ground: Life

From 40 to 4 B.C. a godless Edomite named Herod reigned in cooperation with Rome and brought even deeper affliction to Judah. It was out of this setting that Jesus was born, "a tender shoot, and like a root out of parched ground" (Isaiah 53:2).

Early in the history of God's people, God promised Abraham, "Your reward shall be great" (Genesis 15:1). Abraham and his descendants were to continue to live in obedience. Though God brought forth a chosen people from Abraham's seed, Israel was disobedient in the years that followed, and as we have seen, six foreign nations were allowed to rule over them. Still, despite the bondage God's people suffered as a whole, the obedience of a few was always rewarded. God was faithful to His covenant with Abraham and indeed granted the greatest reward of all: His Son, Jesus. In the meantime, He graciously intervened in the lives of various men and women to prepare His people for the Messiah. For example, He brought life to four childless women so that His redemptive plan could be fulfilled:

Isaac was born to Sarah (Genesis 11-21)

Jacob and Esau were born to Rebekah (Genesis 25)

Samuel was born to Hannah (1 Samuel 1)

John the Baptist was born to Elizabeth (Luke 1)

God also intervened on several occasions to protect the lives of individuals because of the obedience of someone to His Word:

Isaac was spared through God's provision of the sacrificial ram (Genesis 22)

The Holiness and Honor of Praise

David was rescued from Saul's plots with Jonathan's help (1 Samuel 20)

Jehoshaphat's life was saved when Ahab's scheme was thwarted (2 Chronicles 18)

Again and again the Lord preserved His people and readied them for the coming Promise. When His Son was born, a dramatic posture of praise, coupled with divine power, was also born, which was to restore the relationship man had lost with God the Father.

A Promise Worthy of Praise

From the moment Gabriel announced to Mary she would give birth to God's only Son, praise spontaneously flowed from the hearts of all who heard. Mary, Elizabeth, the shepherds, the angels, and Simeon each praised the Lord for very different reasons—but all praised Him.

Mary was full of appreciation for God's majesty and because He had chosen her to be the vessel through whom His Son would be born. This Jesus, "the image of the invisible God, the firstborn of all creation" (Colossians 1:15), in whom "all the fulness [should] dwell" (Colossians 1:19), and in whom "the fulness of Deity dwells in bodily form" (Colossians 2:9), would humble himself as a man in order to restore full fellowship between God and man.

In unexpected moment of glory the archangel Gabriel appeared to Mary and said:

> He will be great, and will be called the Son of the Most High; and the Lord God will give Him the throne of His father David. And He will reign over the house of Jacob

Captivity and Deliverance

forever, and His kingdom will have no end.

Luke 1:32-33

Mary's faith in God took precedence over the seemingly impossible, and she praised Him for His great mercy:

> My soul exalts the Lord, and my spirit has rejoiced in God my Savior. For He has regard for the humble state of His bondslave; for behold, from this time on all generations will count me blessed. For the Mighty One has done great things for me; and holy is His name. And His mercy is upon generation after generation towards those who fear Him. He has done mighty deeds with His arm; He has scattered those who were proud in the thoughts of their heart. He has brought down rulers from their thrones, and has exalted those who were humble. He has filled the hungry with good things; and sent away the rich empty-handed. He has given help to Israel His servant, in remembrance of His mercy, as He spoke to our fathers, to Abraham and his offspring forever.

Luke 1:46-55

Generations have indeed called Mary blessed for her willing spirit.

Elizabeth was pregnant when she heard Mary was going to have a child. The news of this special birth evoked joy from the baby inside her womb and praise from her own spirit.

The Holiness and Honor of Praise

> Blessed among women are you, and blessed is the fruit of your womb! And how has it happened to me, that the mother of my Lord should come to me? For behold, when the sound of your greeting reached my ears, the baby leaped in my womb for joy. And blessed is she who believed that there would be a fulfillment of what had been spoken to her by the Lord.
> Luke 1:42-45

The angels also rejoiced at the news of Christ's birth. From the beginning the angels of the Lord have known His sovereign character, carried out His Word and served Him faithfully. As Psalm 103:20-22 says:

> Bless the Lord, you His angels, mighty in strength, who perform His word, obeying the voice of His word! Bless the Lord, all you His hosts, you who serve Him, doing His will. Bless the Lord, all you works of His, in all places of His dominion; bless the Lord, O my soul!

Because the angels had stood in the holy presence of the Lord and experienced His eternal Truth, it was their delight and privilege to announce His coming to humble shepherds, saying:

> Glory to God in the highest, and on earth peace among men with whom He is pleased.
> Luke 2:14

The shepherds had witnessed this supernatural visit from the heavenly host and thus found Jesus lying in a manger, just as the angels had said.

Captivity and Deliverance

> And when they had seen this, they made known the statement which had been told them about this Child. And all who heard it wondered at the things which were told them by the shepherds. But Mary treasured up all these things, pondering them in her heart. And the shepherds went back, glorifying and praising God for all that they had heard and seen, just as has been told them.
>
> Luke 2:17-20

Simeon, on the other hand, was "righteous and devout, looking for the consolation of Israel," which had been in physical and spiritual bondage for years. The Holy Spirit revealed to him that "he would not see death before he had seen the Lord's Christ" (see Luke 2:25-35). In an attitude of worship he saw the Child Jesus and, taking Him in his arms, he blessed God and said:

> Now Lord, Thou dost let Thy bond-servant depart in peace, according to Thy word; for mine eyes have seen Thy salvation, which Thou hast prepared in the presence of all peoples, a light of revelation to the Gentiles, and the glory of Thy people Israel.
>
> Luke 2:25-32

Jesus, our Deliverer, has come to set us free from the bonds of sin and all forms of captivity. We are set free to praise God forever!

Chapter 5
Reasons for Praise: God's Worthiness

Man has always tried to reach beyond himself to grasp the secrets of life. Since that day in Eden when Adam and Eve ate from the Tree of Knowledge of Good and Evil until today, man has failed to find conclusive, eternal answers on his own. Man's intelligence has taken him to the outer edges of space and time and to the innermost recesses of his own mind. Through his discoveries he has learned how to make educated guesses about life's purpose, but somehow he has missed the point.

Tragically, in the midst of perhaps the most advanced civilization we also find a powerless, defeated church. It is a perplexing truth that man simply cannot grasp anything of eternal value, no matter how religious he is, unless God reveals it to him. As 1 Corinthians 1:27-29 says, "God has chosen the foolish things of the world to shame the wise, and God has chosen the weak things of the world to shame the things which are strong and the base things of the world and the despised, God has chosen, the things that are not, that He might nullify the things that are, that no man should boast before God."

Thus, in His infinite wisdom God chose to reveal himself to man gradually, little by little. Through four distinct names, disclosed during specific times of need, He revealed aspects of His holy character. We will look at these in the following pages.

Jehovah Elohim: The Eternal, Supreme, Mighty, Triune, Creator God

The first revelation of God was to Adam and Eve in the Garden. It was there that man was given dominion over all creation and was instructed to care for it. God gave Adam both life and freedom. He also gave him companionship in Eve. In return, God wanted Adam's love and obedience. He wanted man to know He is the supreme and eternal Creator, and besides Him there is no other god.

> Then God (*Elohim*), said, "Let Us make man in Our image, according to Our likeness; and let them rule over the fish of the sea and over the birds of the sky and over the cattle and over all the earth, and over every creeping thing that creeps on the earth."
>
> Genesis 1:26

> To you it was shown that you might know that the Lord (*Jehovah*), He is God (*Elohim*); there is no other besides Him. . . . Know therefore today, and take it to your heart, that the Lord (*Jehovah*), He is God (*Elohim*) in heaven above and on the earth below; there is no other.
>
> Deuteronomy 4:35, 39

Reasons for Praise: God's Worthiness

God also revealed himself to Noah as *Elohim* and instilled within him His own creativity as He instructed Noah to build an ark of salvation. He mirrored God's nature by constructing a vessel large enough to support his family and pairs of every animal for many days and nights. Through this picture God showed man He would save him out of a dying world and call him to a new life of fruition.

Adonai: Lord, Sovereign Controller, Supreme Ruler

In Genesis 15 *Elohim* appeared to Abram in a vision and promised to bless him. In that moment another aspect of God's character was revealed to man. In addition to being the Triune Creator, He was now recognized as the one sovereign Judge and Ruler.

> After these things the word of the Lord (*Elohim*) came to Abram in a vision, saying, "Do not fear, Abram, I am a shield to you; your reward shall be very great." And Abram said, "O Lord God (*Adonai*), what wilt Thou give me, since I am childless, and the heir of my house is Eliezer of Damascus?"
>
> Genesis 15:1-2

The realization of God's sovereignty in every situation will produce praise within the heart of the believer. As David said in Psalm 86:6-10:

> Give ear, O Lord (*Jehovah*), to my prayer; and give heed to the voice of my supplications! In the day of my trouble I shall call upon Thee, for Thou wilt answer me. There is no one like

The Holiness and Honor of Praise

> Thee among the gods, O Lord (*Adonai*); nor are there any works like Thine. All nations whom Thou has made shall come and worship before Thee, O Lord (*Adonai*); and they shall glorify Thy name. For Thou art great and doest wondrous deeds; Thou alone art God (*Elohim*).

During the Midianite oppression, God revealed himself to Gideon as *Adonai,* the sovereign Controller. He urged him to continue in strength, saying, "I will be with you, and you shall defeat Midian (Hebrew, meaning, 'strife and discord') as one man" (Judges 6:16). Although Gideon fully expected to die in the awesome presence of a righteous Lord, God spoke peace to him instead. Thus, Gideon built an altar to honor the name of *Yahweh-Shalom,* the "Lord of Grace and Peace." Afterwards, he fought the Midianites with only three hundred men, and in the strength of God's might, he won the victory.

El Shaddai: The God of Strength and Personal Blessing

God promised Abram a legacy of blessing which would affect all of humanity and bring glory to Him. Yet, Sarai, his wife, had not received the same personal revelation. She had not been able to bear Abram a child even in her youth, so she never considered the possibility of giving birth in her old age. Evidently, she had no trouble believing God could work a miracle with her husband who was even older, but she had difficulty believing God would be *El Shaddai* in her own life. As a result, Sarai provided Abram with Hagar, her handmaiden, by whom Ishmael was born. The outcome of her effort, of course, was a work of the flesh and therefore completely out of

Reasons for Praise: God's Worthiness

the realm of God's promise. So, to demonstrate His sovereignty in the situation, God appeared to Abram again when he was ninety-nine years old and said:

> "I am God Almighty (*El Shaddai*); walk before Me and be blameless. And *I will* establish My covenant between Me and you, and *I will* multiply you exceedingly." And Abram fell on his face and God (*Elohim*) talked with him, saying, "As for Me, behold, My covenant is with you, and you shall be the father of a multitude of nations. No longer shall your name be called Abram, but your name shall be Abraham; for *I will* make you exceedingly fruitful, and *I will* make nations of you, and kings shall come forth from you. And *I will* establish My covenant between Me and you and your descendants after you throughout their generations for an everlasting covenant, to be God (*Elohim*) to you and to your descendants after you. And *I will* give to you and to your descendants after you, the land of your sojournings, all the land of Canaan, for an everlasting possession; and *I will* be their God (*Elohim*)" (italics added).
>
> Genesis 17:1-8

Despite Sarai's unbelief, God blessed her as well and brought forth the promised son of covenant, Isaac.

> Then God (*Elohim*) said to Abraham, "As for Sarai your wife, you shall not call her name Sarai, but Sarah shall be her name. And *I will*

The Holiness and Honor of Praise

> bless her, and indeed *I will* give you a son by her. Then I will bless her, and she shall be a mother of nations; kings of people shall come from her."
>
> Genesis 17:15-16 (italics added)

Abraham's revelation of God as *El Shaddai*, the God of personal blessing and strength, was shown in yet another way. In a moment of complete yieldedness he was asked to offer Isaac on the altar. Up to that point, no one had been required to make such a sacrifice, and Abraham had to be endowed with a strength beyond himself to carry it through. He had to know God was committed to His covenant and that He would raise his son from the dead if necessary to fulfill His promise. It is this story which reminds us that *El Shaddai* sacrificed His own Son of promise to bring Life and eternal strength and blessing to each of us.

El Shaddai, the God of strength and personal blessing, will perform the impossible to accomplish His will in the lives of His covenant people. Isaac and Jacob discovered God to be *El Shaddai*, as Exodus 6:2-3 records, and when the reality of His character strikes home within our hearts, we too will be changed.

Yahweh: the Unchangeable Lord of Hosts, the God of Grace

In his book, *Systematic Theology*,* Louis Berkhof explains the significance of the holiest name ever used for God:

---

* Louis Berkhof, *Introduction to Systematic Theology*, (Grand Rapids, MI: Baker Books, 1979),

Reasons for Praise: God's Worthiness

> It is especially in the name Yahweh, which gradually supplanted earlier names, that God reveals himself as the God of grace. It has always been regarded as the most sacred and most distinctive name of God, the incommunicable name. The Jews had a superstitious dread of using is, since they read, "He that nameth the name of Yahweh shall surely be put to death" (Leviticus 24:16) . . . they substituted for it either Adonai or Elohim. The Pentateuch connects the name with the Hebrew verb *hayah*, "to be," found in Exodus 3:13-14. The meaning is explained in that scripture, which is rendered, "I Am that I Am," or "I shall be what I shall be." Thus interpreted, the name points to the unchangeableness of God. Yet it is not so much the unchangeableness of His essential Being that is in view, as the unchangeableness of His relationship to His people. The name contains the assurance that God will be for the people of Moses' day what He was for their fathers, Abraham, Isaac, and Jacob. It stresses the covenant faithfulness of God, (and) is His proper name par excellence. . . .

God first introduced himself to Moses in Exodus 3 "in a blazing fire from the midst of a bush" (verse 2). Awestruck, Moses moved closer to see "this marvelous sight" and heard the voice of the Lord, saying:

> Do not come near here; remove your sandals from your feet, for the place on which you are standing is holy ground. . . . I am the God of

The Holiness and Honor of Praise

> your father, the God of Abraham, the God of Isaac, and the God of Jacob.
>
> Exodus 3:5-6

Moses hid his face because he was afraid to look at the eternal Creator. Yet, *Elohim* was also the sovereign Controller and a God of strength and personal blessing. He had heard the cry of His people and was now prepared to rescue them from captivity.

As a young prince in Egypt, Moses saw the tremendous oppression Israel suffered. He tried in the flesh to avenge the wrong he witnessed and had killed an Egyptian. But now he was standing on a mountain with the Lord of Hosts. It was clear that if Moses were going to return to Egypt as God's deliverer, he needed to know *Elohim* was also *Yahweh*, the God of mercy and grace.

> Then Moses said to God, "Behold, I am going to the sons of Israel, and I shall say to them, 'The God of your fathers has sent me to you.' Now they may say to me, 'What is His name?' What shall I say to them?" And God said to Moses, "I AM WHO I AM (*Yahweh*)"; and He said, "Thus you shall say to the sons of Israel, 'I AM has sent me to you.' " And God . . . said to Moses, "Thus you shall say to the sons of Israel, 'The Lord, the God of your fathers, the God of Abraham, the God of Isaac, and the God of Jacob, has sent me to you.' This is My name forever, and this is My memorial-name to all generations."
>
> Exodus 3:13-15

Reasons for Praise: God's Worthiness

This was the fullest revelation God had ever given of himself. To Abraham, Isaac and Jacob, He was *El Shaddai,* but to Moses He became much more: a God of compassion, who took pity on a people who barely knew Him.

It is this same revelation God wants man to experience today. The Greek word, "Jesus," finds its root in the Hebrew, *hayah,* from which *YHWH,* or *Yahweh,* is derived. In essence, Jesus is *Yahweh's* personal name.

> Therefore also God highly exalted Him, and bestowed on Him the name which is above every name, that at the name of Jesus every knee should bow, of those who are in heaven, and on earth, and under the earth, and that every tongue should confess that Jesus Christ is Lord (in Greek, "the supreme authority"), to the glory of God the Father.
>
> Philippians 2:9-11

Fourteen hundred years after Moses, Jesus the Deliverer came to set the captives free, once for all. Like Moses, He came in the name and authority of the eternal God; unlike Moses, this Deliverer was himself *Yahweh,* clothed in human form.

> Philip said to him, "Lord, show us the Father, and it is enough for us." Jesus said to him, "Have I been so long with you, and yet you have not come to know Me, Philip? He who has seen Me has seen the Father. . . ."
>
> John 14:8-9

The Holiness and Honor of Praise

"Your father Abraham rejoiced to see My day; and he saw it, and was glad." The Jews therefore said to Him, "You are not yet fifty years old, and have You seen Abraham?" Jesus said to them, "Truly, truly, I say to you, before Abraham was born, I AM."

John 8:56-58

Thus, the four names of God which describe His character are fulfilled in the person of Jesus. The Bible presents eight other names applicable to our Lord which reveals His nature through the specific ways He meets our needs:

Jirah	Provider	Genesis 22:8-9	John 1:29
Rophe	Healer	Psalm 103:3	1 Peter 2:24
Nissi	Standard	Exodus 17:15	John 12:32
Shalom	Peace	Judges 6:24	Ephesians 2:14-16
Rohi	Shepherd	Psalm 23:1	John 10:11
Tsidkenu	Righteousness	Leviticus 11:45	2 Corinthians 5:21
Shammah	Presence	Psalm 139	Matthew 28:20
M'Kaddesh	Sanctification	Leviticus 20:7	Ephesians 4:24

We can only respond to God as He reveals himself to us. Our Lord is a God of great mercy, and He is faithful to show us both His character and nature in time to prepare us for trials we may face. In sickness, He is already Healer. In distress, He is Peace. In the hopelessness of our sin, He is Perfect Righteousness and Sanctification. Only when we see His total provision will we begin to respond appropriately to our own circumstances.

Chapter 6
Other Reasons for Praise: Authority and Freedom

As God reveals himself to us we see not only who He is but also who we are: sinners saved by grace. In fact, it is only when we acknowledge our need that we can begin to receive the fullness of Christ, that is, His authority and freedom.

> But as many as received, (Greek, "experienced") Him, to them He gave the right to become children of God, even to those who believe in His name.
>
> John 1:12

Perhaps the most significant truth regarding our position in Christ is that He has given us His sovereign authority over Satan and all his demonic forces.

> And the seventy returned with joy, saying, "Lord, even the demons are subject to us in Your name." And He said to them, "I was watching Satan fall from heaven like lightning.

> Behold, I have given you authority to tread upon serpents and scorpions, and over all the power of the enemy, and nothing shall injure you. Nevertheless, do not rejoice in this, that the spirits are subject to you, but rejoice that your names are recorded in heaven."
>
> Luke 10:17-20

The Son of God gave His disciples authority. The Greek translation for "authority" here means "the lawful right, privilege, and superhuman delegated strength."

This power enabled them to "tread upon serpents and scorpions." The Greek word for "serpent" means "a snake with sharp vision, a sly, cunning and artfully malicious person: Satan." "Scorpion" means "to pierce or sting," and its root means "skeptic." Our authority is not only over Satan but also over the sting of the skeptic whose words may pierce our hearts whenever God's Word is challenged. (See Ezekiel 2:3-6.)

In His wisdom, God has put great meaning into simple prepositions to convey His supreme power. Luke 10:19 says we "tread *upon* serpents and scorpions, and *over* all the powers of the enemy" (italics added). The word "upon" is from the Greek *eperotema*, which means "answer." The word "over" comes from the Greek *epi*, which means "the superimposition of time, place and order of something which comes to rest on something else." When the enemy comes against the people of God, he can be met with divine answers, declared in holy authority as God superimposes His power over time, place and order, bringing it to rest on His people. Neither Satan nor

Other Reasons for Praise: Authority and Freedom

---

his demons have any control over the Christian who walks in faith.

This word, *epi*, used in the accusative tense, appears frequently in the Scriptures (Matthew 3:16; Acts 1:8, James 5:14-15; and Luke 1:35). It is used over fifty times in the New Testament, always in power-packed situations in which God superimposes His will over man's time, place and order.

In Luke 10:17-20, Jesus is telling His disciples that God will move through them to "cover over" Satan's power with His own, greater power. It is important to remember that the enemy has power, or *dunamis,* which is generally associated with the explosive power of the Holy Spirit. The point here, however, is that God is *all-powerful.* He has allowed Satan to exercise a certain degree of power to show that He is indeed sovereign. Any authority we possess is found *only* in our relationship with the Lord.

Jesus' Response: Praise

>At that very time He rejoiced greatly in the Holy Spirit, and said, "I praise Thee, O Father, Lord of heaven and earth, that Thou didst hide these things from the wise and intelligent and didst reveal them to babes. Yes, Father, for thus it was well-pleasing in Thy sight. All things have been handed over to Me by My Father, and no one knows who the Son is except the Father, and who the Father is except the Son, and anyone to whom the Son wills to reveal Him."
>
>Luke 10:21-22

The Holiness and Honor of Praise

It seems the greatest desire among Christians today is to have a balanced walk with the Lord. There is a tendency among some, however, to overreact when they witness a miracle. In Luke 10 Jesus stressed that the power from above is the *by-product* of a right relationship with the Father. Many believers want to experience the supernatural but fail to recognize the importance of a righteous walk. Anointing power is given to those who are true disciples, who hear and obey the Word of the living Lord (Psalm 50:23).

Jesus had found seventy disciples who were indeed willing to hear and obey. With exceeding joy He praised His Father that they were learning how to appropriate their authority and overturn the works of the enemy. Jesus even said He saw Satan fall from heaven like lightning (Luke 10:18). At that very moment the Holy Spirit, by whom Jesus did *all* His miracles, joined with Him in an expression of thankfulness and blessing that the Truth which had been revealed was being received as well. The word "rejoiced" in verse 21 is *agalliao*, meaning "to jump for joy with exceeding gladness and joy, greatly rejoicing." It may be hard to imagine Jesus jumping for joy, but here we see Him totally fulfilled as He watched His own life manifested through "babes."

True praise always produces freedom within our spirit. No matter what the circumstances, praise invites the manifest presence of our Holy God, which can bring freedom to others as well. Look at this story about Paul and Silas:

Other Reasons for Praise: Authority and Freedom

. . . They said, "These men are throwing our city into confusion. . . ." And the crowd rose up together against them, and the chief magistrates tore their robes off them, and proceeded to order them to be beaten with rods. And when they had inflicted many blows upon them, they threw them into prison, commanding the jailer to guard them securely; and he, having received such a command, threw them into the inner prison, and fastened their feet to stocks. But about midnight Paul and Silas were praying and singing hymns of praise to God, and the prisoners were listening to them, and suddenly there came a great earthquake, so that the foundations of the prison house were shaken, and immediately all the doors were opened, and everyone's chains were unfastened. And when the jailer had been roused out of sleep and had seen the prison doors opened, he drew his sword and was about to kill himself, supposing that the prisoners had escaped. But Paul cried out with a loud voice, saying, "Do yourself no harm, for we are all here!" And he called for lights and rushed in and trembling with fear, he fell down before Paul and Silas, and after he brought them out, he said, "Sirs, what must I do to be saved?" And they said, "Believe in the Lord Jesus, and you shall be saved, you and your household."

Acts 16:20-31

The Holiness and Honor of Praise

Prior to his conversion Paul had been a student of the Law. He sat at the feet of Gamaliel, a great teacher and Pharisee whose influence affected the Sanhedrin (Acts 5:34-40; 22:3). Saul, as he was called then, understood the Hebrew writings, and he obeyed them. Of himself, he said he was:

> . . . circumcised the eighth day, of the nation of Israel, of the tribe of Benjamin, a Hebrew of Hebrews; as to the Law, a Pharisee; as to zeal, a persecutor of the church; as to the righteousness which is in the Law, found blameless.
>
> Philippians 3:5-6

Saul was a man filled with the letter of the Law but not the Spirit of the Law; however, it was the Spirit of Jesus who confronted him on the road to Damascus and turned his life around. Blinded by the glory of the Lord, his religious zeal vanished. He found himself totally dependent on the compassion of those around him, and especially on the obedience of a man named Ananias. An attitude of prayer and fasting settled upon him, driving him to the desert. For three years he communed with God, and it was through this encounter that the *logos* became *rhema*, the revealed word. Jesus so captivated his heart that Saul became a new man: Paul. He discovered true freedom and saw that chains could never bind his spirit, for he had become a prisoner of the Lord.

> Therefore, do not be ashamed of the testimony of our Lord, or of me His prisoner; but join with me in suffering for the gospel according to the power of God.
>
> 2 Timothy 1:8

Other Reasons for Praise: Authority and Freedom

This is why Paul and Silas could praise God so freely in the Philippian jail. Although he lived in New Testament times, Paul's training had been in Hebrew. He knew that *Yadah* was the extending of his hands in praise, open and upward to God, acknowledging His power. He understood that *halal* meant "to boast in the works of God." He knew *towdah* meant "to show God adoration with the uplifted hand." All the Hebrew words for praise had taken on real meaning since his conversion.

Acts 16:25 says that at about midnight Paul and Silas began to pray and sing praises to the Lord. Their words filled the jail, and the other prisoners listened. But God also heard and was ready to move in response to their petitions and praise. It had been a very dark situation, but they invited God to invade time and space with His strength and grace. Thus, God shook the earth with such force that doors of the inner prison were thrown open and "everyone's chains were unfastened."

Indeed, Paul and Silas sang hymns of praise (Greek, *humneo;* Hebrew, *tehillah*) to the Lord. It is significant that both their prayers and praise were directed *to* God, not simply about Him to others. In this sense, their songs took the form of *ainos,* "laudation." The Greek root of this word can be traced once again to *epi* in the accusative tense, "the superimposition of time, place and order of something which comes to rest on something else." It was the superimposition of God in that midnight hour that not only opened the doors and loosed the chains but brought rest to those who had been bound.

Realizing the penalty for allowing prisoners to escape, the jailer was ready to kill himself when he saw that the doors had been opened, but Paul assured him that all

The Holiness and Honor of Praise

the prisoners had remained in their cells. With this the jailer's life had been saved, but more than that, he was now willing to be saved spiritually. Praise brought the presence of God, and His presence always brings conviction of sin. When man's heart is yielded to the Lord, true freedom will result.

> Yet Thou art holy, O Thou who art enthroned upon the praises of Israel.
>
> Psalm 22:3

> . . . I saw the Lord sitting on a throne, lofty and exalted, with the train of His robe filling the temple. . . . Then I said, "Woe is me, for I am ruined! Because I am a man of unclean lips; for my eyes have seen the King, the Lord of hosts."
>
> Isaiah 6:1, 5

Chapter 7
God's Picture of Worship: The Tabernacle

God is Spirit, and true worship is communion of our spirit with His. Worship is an intimate experience as seen in the Greek word *proskuneo,* which means "to kiss, reverence, bow down before, prostrate." God desires His people to worship Him in spirit and in truth (John 4:24).

Long before Calvary, God gave the world a picture of worship in the wilderness. The Tabernacle showed how man could come into His presence and fellowship with Him in the purest sense. God's design for the Tabernacle was very specific, because it was to represent some fundamental truths: God is holy and, apart from the shedding of blood, man's sin forever separates him from the Lord. The Tabernacle also speaks of God's mercy and provision so that man may know forgiveness and intimacy with the Lord God.

The Holiness and Honor of Praise

The Door

> I am the door; if anyone enters through Me, he shall be saved, and shall go in and out, and find pasture.
>
> John 10:9

The Eastern door of the Tabernacle led into the courtyard and was draped with blue, purple, scarlet, and fine linen cloth. These colors are sprinkled throughout the Bible and symbolize Jesus' deity, royalty, sacrifice, and complete humanity. They also represent the four gospels where these truths about Christ are fully explained:

John	The Incarnate God	John 1:1-5, 9-18; 6:46
Matthew	The Kingdom Message	Matthew 4:23; 5:7
Mark	The Willing Servant	Mark 1:9-11; 3:31-35
Luke	The Perfect Man	Luke 5:29-32; 7:11-15

The door to the Tabernacle, like the spiritual door to salvation, was wide and open, reminding us that "whosoever will may come."

The Altar

> But when Christ appeared as a high priest of the good things to come, He entered through the greater and more perfect tabernacle, not made with hands, that is to say, not of this creation; and not through the blood of goats and calves, but through His own blood, He entered the holy place once for all, having obtained eternal redemption.
>
> Hebrews 9:11-12

God's Picture of Worship: The Tabernacle

> I urge you therefore, brethren, by the mercies of God, to present your bodies a living and holy sacrifice, acceptable to God, which is your spiritual service of worship.
>
> Romans 12:1

Once inside the Tabernacle the first thing we encounter is a brazen altar, symbolizing God's judgment of sin. The altar was square, five cubits long and five cubits wide, made of wood and overlayed with brass or copper. It was at the altar that sin was judged, and it was at the altar sin was paid for. Thus, the very instrument of judgment became the instrument of mercy as well. As the priest laid hands on the sacrificial animal, man's sin was transfered to it. Then, as the animal's blood was shed, the sin was covered and thus judged. Finally, fire from the altar consumed all evidence of sin, creating for man a sense of holy freedom.

The altar was open at the top and bottom and had a horn on each of the upper corners (Exodus 27:1-2). The sides faced north, south, east, and west, indicating that God's immeasurable grace reaches to the four corners of the earth (Ezekiel 43:15-17; Romans 8:38-39).

Fire from the altar was also used to keep the golden candlestick and incense continually lit. Likewise, the Cross is our salvation and source of Light as we minister before the Lord.

The Laver

> ... Christ also loved the church and gave Himself up for her; that He might sanctify her, having cleansed her by the washing of the

The Holiness and Honor of Praise

> water with the word, that He might present to
> Himself the church in all her glory, having no
> spot or wrinkle or any such thing; but that she
> should be holy and blameless.
>
> Ephesians 5:25b-27

Beyond the altar of sacrifice was the laver where physical cleansing took place. This special basin was made from the molded bronze mirrors of the women who served at the Tent of Meeting (Exodus 38:8).

All the priests were required to wash before they could carry out their duties. First Peter 2:9 says we are priests of the New Covenant, and we can only approach God after we have been justified at the Cross and washed by the Word.

> Do you not know that the unrighteous shall
> not inherit the kingdom of God? . . . And such
> were some of you; but you were washed, but
> you were sanctified, but you were justified in
> the name of the Lord Jesus Christ, and in the
> Spirit of our God.
>
> 1 Corinthians 6:9a, 11

> Let us draw near with a sincere heart in full
> assurance of faith, having our hearts sprinkled
> clean from an evil conscience and our body
> washed with pure water.
>
> Hebrews 10:22

Whereas the altar represents the sacrifice Christ made once for all, the laver represents the continuous washing we receive from God's Word. It is interesting that the laver was made from mirrors. The Word of God acts as

God's Picture of Worship: The Tabernacle

a mirror today, showing us the reflection of His glory in our lives:

> But we all, with unveiled face beholding as in a mirror the glory of the Lord, are being transformed into the same image from glory to glory, just as from the Lord, the Spirit.
>
> 2 Corinthians 3:18

The priests were not the only ones, however, to be washed by water from the laver; the sacrifices also had to be cleansed. Here the picture of baptism emerges:

> Or do you not know that all of us who have been baptized into Christ Jesus have been baptized into His death? Therefore we have been buried with Him through baptism into death, in order that as Christ was raised from the dead through the glory of the Father, so we too might walk in newness of life.
>
> Romans 6:3-4

> And corresponding to that, baptism now saves you—not the removal of dirt from the flesh, but an appeal to God for a good conscience—through the resurrection of Jesus Christ.
>
> 1 Peter 3:21

We must not remain at the door, or at the altar, but move on to the laver and then to the other ministries God has ordained to bring us into His presence.

The Holiness and Honor of Praise

The Candlestick

> Again therefore Jesus spoke to them, saying, "I am the light of the world; he who follows Me shall not walk in darkness, but shall have the light of life."
>
> John 8:12

> You are the light of the world. A city set on a hill cannot be hidden. Nor do men light a lamp and put it under the peck-measure, but on the lampstand; and it gives light to all who are in the house. Let your light shine before men in such a way that they may see your good works, and glorify your Father who is in heaven.
>
> Matthew 5:14-16

As we enter the Holy Place and look to the left, we see the golden candlestick, which was an ornate oil holder made of beaten gold. It was comprised of a center shaft with three branches coming out of each side. The word "shaft" in the Hebrew is *yarek*, meaning, "thigh, loin, side or base." The candlestick represents Christ and the Church, which comes forth from His side.

> I am the vine, you are the branches; he who abides in Me, and I in him, he bears much fruit; for apart from Me you can do nothing.
>
> John 15:5

The cups at the top of the shaft and stems were filled with oil, symbolizing God's Holy Spirit, who fills us individually and collectively.

> . . . You were formerly darkness, but now you are light in the Lord; walk as children of

God's Picture of Worship: The Tabernacle

> light (for the fruit of the light consists in all goodness and righteousness and truth), trying to learn what is pleasing to the Lord.
>
> Ephesians 5:8-10

> If we walk in the light as He Himself is in the light, we have fellowship with one another, and the blood of Jesus His Son cleanses us from all sin.
>
> 1 John 1:7

God's Spirit illumines our minds so we can understand more fully some of His great mysteries.

> But the Helper, the Holy Spirit, whom the Father will send in My name, He will teach you all things, and bring to your remembrance all that I said to you.
>
> John 14:26

> "Things which eye has not seen and ear has not heard, and which have not entered the heart of man, all that God has prepared for those who love Him." For to us God revealed them through the Spirit; for the Spirit searches all things, even the depths of God.
>
> 1 Corinthians 2:9-10

The cups that held the oil were fashioned after almond buds and blossoms, which typify our growth and fruitfulness and are the natural results of a life filled with the Spirit.

Since the Tabernacle walls were covered with thick skins, the only source of light was the candlestick. The priests had to trim the wicks and add fresh oil every

The Holiness and Honor of Praise

day at twilight, or else the flame would flicker and go out (Exodus 30:8). Likewise, we who are lightbearers must walk in the Spirit to make sure our light does not go out, which would leave us unprepared for the Lord's coming.

> Then the kingdom of heaven will be comparable to ten virgins, who took their lamps, and went out to meet the bridegroom. And five of them were foolish, and five were prudent. For when the foolish took their lamps, they took no oil with them, but the prudent took oil in flasks along with their lamps. Now while the bridegroom was delaying, they all got drowsy and began to sleep. But at midnight there was a shout, "Behold, the bridegroom! Come out to meet him." Then all those virgins arose, and trimmed their lamps. And the foolish said to the prudent, "Give us some of your oil, for our lamps are going out." But the prudent answered, saying, "No, there will not be enough for us and you too; go instead to the dealers and buy some for yourselves." And while they were going away to make the purchase, the bridegroom came, and those who were ready went in with him to the wedding feast; and the door was shut. And later the other virgins also came, saying, "Lord, Lord, open up for us." But he answered and said, "Truly I say to you, I do not know you." Be on the alert then, for you do not know the day nor the hour.
> Matthew 25:1-13

God's Picture of Worship: The Tabernacle

The Table of Shewbread

> Truly, truly, I say to you, he who believes has eternal life. I am the bread of life. Your fathers ate the manna in the wilderness, and they died. This is the bread which comes down out of heaven, so that one may eat of it and not die. I am the living bread that comes down out of heaven; if any one eats of this bread, he shall live forever; and the bread also which I shall give for the life of the world is My flesh.
>
> John 6:47-51

Directly across from the candlestick was the table of shewbread, which represents communion with God. Here we take into ourselves the very life of God. This is a kind of intimacy which naturally produces light in the world through works that honor the Lord.

There were twelve loaves of bread on the table for the twelve tribes of Israel. Thus, God showed His people there is always enough of Him to nourish us all. The word "shewbread" comes from two Hebrew words, *panim*, which means "face," and *lechem*, meaning "bread, food, grain." Shewbread, in its truest sense, implies a continual feeding on the personality and attitudes of God.

> And while they were eating, Jesus took some bread, and after a blessing, He broke it and gave it to the disciples, and said, "Take, eat; this is My body."
>
> Matthew 26:26

Only the priests were allowed to eat the shewbread in the Tabernacle. As New Testament covenant priests, we, too, are invited to feed on the Bread of Life.

The Holiness and Honor of Praise

Ho! Every one who thirsts, come to the waters; and you who have no money come, buy and eat. Come, buy wine and milk without money and without cost. Why do you spend money for what is not bread, and your wages for what does not satisfy? Listen carefully to me, and eat what is good, and delight yourself in abundance. Incline your ear and come to Me. Listen, that you may live; and I will make an everlasting covenant with you, according to the faithful mercies shown to David. Behold, I have made him a witness to the peoples, a leader and commander for the peoples. Behold, you will call a nation you do not know, and a nation which knows you not will run to you, because of the Lord your God, even the Holy One of Israel; for He has glorified you.

Isaiah 55:1-5

Is not the cup of blessing which we bless a sharing in the blood of Christ? Is not the bread which we break a sharing in the body of Christ? Since there is one bread, we who are many are one body; for we all partake of the one bread.

1 Corinthians 10:16-17

For as often as you eat this bread and drink the cup, you proclaim the Lord's death until He comes.

1 Corinthians 11:26

Let us therefore celebrate the feast, not with old leaven, nor with the leaven of malice and wickedness, but with the unleavened bread of sincerity and truth.

1 Corinthians 5:8

God's Picture of Worship: The Tabernacle

The Altar of Incense

> May my prayer be counted as incense before
> Thee; the lifting up of my hands as the evening
> offering.
>
> Psalm 141:2

Directly in front of the curtain which led into the Holy of Holies stood the altar of incense. This altar was made of acacia wood and overlayed with pure gold. It was here that the priest burned fragrant incense every morning and evening at twilight when the lamps were trimmed. (Read Exodus 30:34-38.)

The spices that made up the incense paint a vivid picture of our life in Christ. Stacte in Hebrew is *nataph*, meaning "drop." Its root means "to speak by inspiration." Onycha comes from *shecheleth*, meaning "peeling off scales." Galbanum is from the Hebrew word *chelbenah*, meaning "the choicest part, or fruitfulness." Yet, each of these spices was to be mixed with frankincense, which comes from *lebownah*, meaning "whiteness." Our walk before the Lord is to consist of inspiration, revelation and fruitfulness; however, unless these are combined with holiness, the result is speculation, knowledge, and works.

The incense was to be salted, or tempered, which means each part had to be crushed and thoroughly mixed together. God may allow us to be crushed through various trials so we will grow stronger in *His* might. We tend to be self-reliant in all situations, but God wants us to trust Him in everything. Therefore, He sometimes allows disappointment or tragedy to come our way. God wants to get our attention so He can fill the gaps in our lives as they should be filled, and we must learn to accept the heavy side

The Holiness and Honor of Praise

of His hand in addition to the side that pours out blessings. We should remember, too, that "a bruised reed He will not break, and a dimly burning wick He will not extinguish; He will faithfully bring forth justice" (Isaiah 42:3).

Whenever inspiration, revelation, fruitfulness, and holiness are combined in the life of a Christian, the predominant ingredient will always be holiness, which reflects God's character. Only then can we commune with Him as He desires.

It was a holy fire that consumed the incense and produces the pleasing aroma which filled the Tabernacle. As Hebrews 12:29 says, "our God is a consuming fire." It is His holiness which burns up the "wood, hay, and straw" in our lives to reveal those things we have built on a foundation of "gold, silver, and precious stones" (1 Corinthians 3:12).

> Each man's work will become evident; for the day will show it, because it is to be revealed with fire; and the fire itself will test the quality of each man's work.
>
> 1 Corinthians 3:13

The incense was so integrated in the priest's ministry that on the Day of Atonement he put two handfuls of it on the fire before the Lord, "that the cloud of incense may cover the mercy seat that is on the ark of the testimony . . ." (Leviticus 16:13). Afterwards, he sprinkled blood from the sacrifice on the mercy seat and in front of it to receive forgiveness of sin for himself and the people (see Leviticus 16:11-15).

Revelation 5:8 speaks of "golden bowls full of incense,

God's Picture of Worship: The Tabernacle

which are the prayers of the saints." Indeed, our prayers and praise please the Lord, who sees us covered by the blood of the Lamb. Thus, the fragrance our lives produce makes an impact on the world around us. For some it is an aroma of hope; for others, it is the smell of God's judgment.

> But thanks be to God, who always leads us in His triumph in Christ, and manifests through us the sweet aroma of the knowledge of Him in every place. For we are a fragrance of Christ to God among those who are being saved and among those who are perishing; to the one an aroma from death to death, to the other an aroma from life to life.
>
> 2 Corinthians 2:14-16

When we determine to live in an attitude of thanksgiving and praise, God ushers us into His presence where we may dwell. In Matthew 27:51 we are told "the veil of the temple was torn in two from top to bottom," granting us access to the Father through Christ's blood. The writer of Hebrews describes the Tabernacle and places the altar of incense *inside* the Holy of Holies with the Ark of the Covenant, unlike the description given in Exodus 30. Since Jesus' death on the cross, we may freely enter into communion with God—through holy praise.

The Holy of Holies
1. The Ark of the Covenant

Of all the pieces in the Tabernacle the Ark was the most significant in portraying God's supreme holiness. It contained the testimony, or Law, which Moses received on

The Holiness and Honor of Praise

Mount Sinai, as well as manna that had fallen in the desert, and Aaron's rod which budded as a sign of his priestly authority (Hebrews 9:4).

The Ark is a beautiful picture of God's unchanging character. He is completely righteous, able to meet our every need, and willing to delegate His authority to those who abide in His presence.

2. The Mercy Seat

O, Lord, Thou didst show favor to Thy land;
Thou didst restore the captivity of Jacob.
Thou didst forgive the iniquity of Thy people;
Thou didst cover all their sin.
Thou didst withdraw all Thy fury;
Thou didst turn away from Thy burning anger.
Restore us, O God of our salvation,
And cause Thine indignation toward us to cease.
Wilt Thou be angry with us forever?
Wilt Thou prolong Thine anger to all generations?
Wilt Thou not Thyself revive us again,
That Thy people may rejoice in Thee?
Show us Thy lovingkindness, O Lord,
And grant us Thy salvation.
I will hear what God the Lord will say;
For He will speak peace to His people,
    to His godly ones;
But let them not turn back to folly.
Surely His salvation is near to those who fear Him,
That glory may dwell in our land.
Lovingkindness and truth have met together;
Righteousness and peace have kissed each other.
Truth springs from the earth;

God's Picture of Worship: The Tabernacle

And righteousness looks down from heaven.
Indeed, the Lord will give what is good;
And our land will yield its produce.
Righteousness will go before Him,
And will make His footsteps into a way.

Psalm 85

The holiness of Almighty God is truly awesome. However, were it not for His abounding mercy, we would all face eternity without a shadow of hope. His divinity cannot help but bring to light our shortcomings, and we are thereby judged. Yet, from the beginning, God's plan included grace. When Adam and Eve sinned, He killed an animal and covered them with its skin. When the entire Old Testament world turned away from Him, He showed Noah how to construct a vessel large enough to save his family and pairs of animals to replenish the earth. When the children of Israel were held captive in Egypt, He heard their cries and sent Moses to lead them out. He desired to teach them His ways and bring them into a land of abundance and peace.

This is repeated again in the Holy of Holies where the mercy seat, representing God's nature, rested above the Ark, symbolizing His character. Here, God's perfect righteousness is united with His perfect mercy to create grace.

"Righteousness" comes from the Hebrew *tsedaqah*, meaning "justice, virtue, prosperity, right-ness"; its root means "to be right in a moral sense or in a court of law." Its Greek translation, *dikaios*, means "to be equitable or fair, whether in character or act, to be innocent and holy." Its root, *diistemi*, means "to stand apart, to remove by

The Holiness and Honor of Praise

intervention." "Mercy," on the other hand, is a picture of God "stooping in kindness to an inferior" (in Hebrew, the word is *chanan*).

Because man was made in the image of God for His good pleasure, any act of willful disobedience is a direct assault on God's holiness. The Lord's righteousness is uncompromising and, therefore, atonement had to be made before man could ever stand in His presence. When Jesus died on the cross, He became not only the atonement God required but the Way by which we could know His mercy.

Through Jesus' death and resurrection a new covenant was established, a covenant based on His faithfulness alone. God knows if we are left to ourselves, we will always fail Him. But when He looks into the heart of the believer and sees the blood of Jesus, He is reminded of His covenant with His Son. This is grace, the work of God through Christ Jesus. It is the only reason we are able to enter into the Holy of Holies and commune with the Father as He intended from the very beginning.

"Grace" comes from the Hebrew word, *chen*, which is rich in meaning. It embraces "graciousness, kindness, favor, beauty, and pleasantness." Its Greek counterpart, *charis*, amplifies the Hebrew by including "the gratifying divine influence upon the heart and its reflection in the life; it is a gift given with liberality, making us acceptable to God."

We have the privilege of responding to God's abounding grace in one of two ways: if lost, we can turn in repentance to complete salvation; if saved, we can move from praise into true worship. Whichever situation we find ourselves in, we can be certain our decision is made all by the grace of God.

God's Picture of Worship: The Tabernacle

But God, being rich in mercy, because of His great love with which He loved us, even when we were dead in our transgressions, made us alive together with Christ (by grace you have been saved), and raised us up with Him, and seated us with Him in the heavenly places, in Christ Jesus, in order that in the ages to come He might show the surpassing riches of His grace in kindness toward us in Christ Jesus. For by grace you have been saved through faith; and that not of yourselves, it is the gift of God; not as a result of works, that no one should boast. For we are His workmanship, created in Christ Jesus for good works, which God prepared beforehand, that we should walk in them.

Ephesians 2:4-10

Chapter 8
Entering Into Worship: The Priest

The Spirit of the Lord God is upon me,
Because the Lord has anointed me
To bring good news to the afflicted;
He has sent me to bind up the brokenhearted,
To proclaim liberty to captives;
And freedom to prisoners;
To proclaim the favorable year of the Lord,
And the day of vengeance of our God;
To comfort all who mourn,
To grant those who mourn in Zion,
Giving them a garland instead of ashes,
The oil of gladness instead of mourning,
The mantle of praise instead of a spirit of fainting.
So they will be called oaks of righteousness,
The planting of the Lord, that He may be glorified. . . .
But you will be called the priests of the Lord;
You will be spoken of as ministers of our God.
You will eat the wealth of nations,

The Holiness and Honor of Praise

And in their riches you will boast.
Instead of your shame you will have a double portion,
And instead of humiliation they will shout for joy over
   their portion.
Therefore they will possess a double portion in their land,
Everlasting joy will be theirs.
For I, the Lord, love justice,
I hate robbery in the burnt offering;
And I will faithfully give them their recompense,
And I will make an everlasting covenant with them.
Then their offspring will be known among the nations,
And their descendants in the midst of the peoples.
All who see them will recognize them
Because they are the offspring whom the Lord has blessed.
I will rejoice greatly in the Lord,
My soul will exult in my God;
For He has clothed me with garments of salvation,
He has wrapped me with a robe of righteousness,
As a bridegroom decks himself with a garland,
And as a bride adorns herself with her jewels.
For as the earth brings forth its sprouts,
And as a garden causes the things sown in it to spring up,
So the Lord God will cause righteousness and praise
To spring up before all the nations.
                                        Isaiah 61:1-3, 6-11

God chose the tribe of Levi to bring forth His priests to minister to Him and His people. The name "Levi" means "attached" and reminds us we are forever attached to Jesus Christ, our High Priest (Hebrews 9:11-15).

God scattered the Levitical priests throughout all the tribes of Israel and gave them no earthly inheritance;

Entering Into Worship: The Priest

instead, He promised He would be their portion (Deuteronomy 18:1-2).

As Israel entered the Promised Land, the tribe of Levi was given forty-eight cities throughout Canaan, including the six cities of refuge to which an offender could flee. As holy priests (1 Peter 2:9), we are to be sprinkled throughout the world to meet needs in the name of Jesus (Matthew 5:13-16). To those needing a special touch from God, we are to offer a place of refuge (Galatians 6:2). Most important, our eyes are not to be on an earthly inheritance, but to be on treasures of the kingdom of God (Matthew 6:19-21).

The Lord God was himself the inheritance of the priests; and He made sure all their needs were met each day. They were given the *best* of the fresh oil, the *best* of the new wine, the *finest* grain and *first* fruits (Numbers 18:12). Jehovah is still the provider for our spiritual, as well as physical, needs:

He has given us His anointing (1 John 2:20)

He has filled us with His Spirit (Ephesians 5:18)

He has fed us with His Word (Matthew 4:4)

He has given us the fruit of His Spirit (Galatians 5:22-23)

In every way God has provided for us and more than adequately equipped us to minister His Truth as holy priests set apart unto Him.

> Not that we are adequate in ourselves to consider anything as coming from ourselves, but our adequacy is from God, who also made

The Holiness and Honor of Praise

us adequate as servants of a new covenant, not of the letter, but of the Spirit; for the letter kills, but the Spirit gives life.

2 Corinthians 3:5-6

The Priestly Garments
> But put on the Lord Jesus Christ, and make no provision for the flesh in regard to its lusts.
>
> Romans 13:14

Before a priest could minister, he had to be properly clothed, and in order to minister before God, he had to put on very special raiment. In these garments the high priest entered the Holy of Holies once a year on the Day of Atonement. Likewise, we enter the Lord's presence through our High Priest, Jesus, to offer up spiritual sacrifices of praise (1 Peter 2:5), clothed in the beauty of holiness (2 Chronicles 20:21; Psalm 29:2).

The Linen Breeches

Since the first day when Adam and Eve sinned in the Garden of Eden, God has provided a covering for sin. In the Tabernacle, He commanded that the priest's nakedness, which represents sin, be covered with linen.

"Nakedness" comes from the Hebrew *ervah*, meaning "shame, disgrace, uncleanness"; its root is *arah*, meaning "to be bare, empty, destitute, uncovered." The root word from which "linen" is taken is *badad* and means "solitude, to be alone, to divide."

When the priest put on the linen breeches, he was in essence declaring that his sin and disgrace had been

Entering Into Worship: The Priest

covered by the blood of the Lamb and he was now set apart to do God's will.

> Blessed are those whose lawless deeds have been forgiven, and whose sins have been covered.
> Romans 4:7

The Linen Tunic
God judged our sin at the cross, and we have put on His righteousness. Just as the linen tunic covered the whole man, we have been *completely* redeemed.

This tunic was worn under the other clothes and symbolizes the inner working of holiness which began when we received our new nature.

> Put on the new self, which in the likeness of God has been created in righteousness and holiness of the truth.
> Ephesians 4:24

The Robe
The priestly robe was made of deep blue material with alternating gold bells and blue, violet and scarlet pomegranates. The bells would ring whenever he entered the Holy of Holies, letting the other priests know he was all right. The pomegranates represent the fruit which grows on an upright tree. Together they symbolize a walk of righteousness. The robe with all its color and decoration typifies the outward, multifaceted expression of an inner work of holiness in the Christian's life. We have been adorned with the robe of righteousness, and the fruit and gifts of the Spirit will be evident as we abide in His presence.

The Holiness and Honor of Praise

Even the one who has strayed from the Lord may be given the robe of righteousness when he repents, as in the story of the prodigal son. When the wayward son grew weary of living in filth, he returned home. His father was overjoyed to see him and commanded that the best robe be brought for his repentant son, thus signifying to the rest of the world his son's total acceptance into the family (Luke 15:11-24).

Isaiah 64:6 says, "All of us have become like one who is unclean, and all our righteous deeds are like a filthy garment. . . ." Our God is a merciful, loving Father, and He has declared:

> Remove the filthy garments. . . . See, I have taken your iniquity away from you and will clothe you with festal robes.
>
> Zechariah 3:4

The Ephod

Over the robe the priest wore an ephod made of gold with blue, purple and scarlet cloth, and fine linen. On each shoulder was a stone set in gold bearing the names of six of the tribes of Israel. "Ephod" literally means "image," and indicates our need to be conformed into the image of Christ. We are only conformed to His image as we abide in His presence; the more time we spend with Him, the more like Him we become. We are changed into people of honor, authority and character.

> . . . with unveiled face beholding as in a mirror the glory of the Lord, (we) are being

Entering Into Worship: The Priest

transformed into the same image from glory to glory, just as from the Lord, the Spirit.
2 Corinthians 3:18

Therefore we do not lose heart, but though our outer man is decaying, yet our inner man is being renewed day by day. For momentary, light affliction is producing for us an eternal weight of glory far beyond all comparison, while we look not at the things which are seen, but at the things which are not seen; for the things which are seen are temporal, but the things which are not seen are eternal.
2 Corinthians 4:16-18

The Girdle
Fitted about the priest's waist was a sash, or girdle. "Sash" literally means "a yoke of servitude, an obligation" and was woven from fine linen and from blue, purple and scarlet cloth.

Ephesians 6:14 says we are obligated to be girded with truth. In biblical days the girdle was part of a soldier's armor and was worn around the middle of the man for balance and protection. As priests unto the Lord we must realize there is no balance or protection apart from the truth of God's Word.

King David seemed to understand a great deal about battling the enemy and being girded with truth. In Psalm 18:37-39 he says:

I pursued my enemies and overtook them, and I did not turn back until they were

The Holiness and Honor of Praise

consumed. I shattered them, so that they were not able to rise; they fell under my feet. For Thou has girded me with strength for battle; Thou hast subdued under me those who rose up against me.

Then in Psalm 30:1, 4, 5, 11, and 12 he says:

> I will extol Thee, O Lord, for Thou hast lifted me up, and hast not let my enemies rejoice over me. . . . Sing praise to the Lord, you His godly ones, and give thanks to His holy name. For His anger is but for a moment, His favor is for a lifetime; weeping may last for the night, but a shout of joy comes in the morning. . . . Thou hast turned for me my mourning into dancing; Thou hast loosed my sackcloth and girded me with gladness; that my soul may sing praise to Thee, and not be silent. O Lord my God, I will give thanks to Thee forever.

Finally in Psalm 65 he says:

> There will be silence before Thee, and praise in Zion, O God; and to Thee the vow will be performed. O Thou who dost hear prayer, to Thee all men come. Iniquities prevail against me; as for our transgressions, Thou dost forgive them. How blessed is the one whom Thou dost choose, and bring near to Thee, to dwell in Thy courts. We will be satisfied with the goodness of Thy house, Thy holy temple. By awesome deeds Thou dost answer

Entering Into Worship: The Priest

us in righteousness, O God of our salvation, Thou who art the trust of all the ends of the earth and of the farthest sea . . .who dost still the roaring of the seas, the roaring of their waves, and the tumult of the peoples. And they who dwell in the ends of the earth stand in awe of Thy signs; Thou dost make the dawn and the sunset shout for joy. Thou dost visit the earth, and cause it to overflow; Thou dost greatly enrich it; the stream of God is full of water; Thou dost prepare their grain, for thus Thou dost prepare the earth. Thou dost water its furrows abundantly; Thou dost settle its ridges; Thou dost soften it with showers; Thou dost bless its growth. Thou hast crowned the year with Thy bounty, and Thy paths drip with fatness. The pastures of the wilderness drip, and the hills gird themselves with rejoicing. The meadows are clothed with flocks, and the valleys are covered with grain; they shout for joy, yes, they sing.

In these three passages we find the truth with which we are to be girded. In Psalm 18:39 we read that David was girded with *strength*. The Hebrew word for "strength" is *chayil,* meaning "a force, whether from man or God, virtue, valor, and wealth." Its root is *chiyl,* meaning "twisted, strength from pain, grief, rest, or joy." David knew God was faithful in all circumstances and that spiritual growth comes from a variety of experiences, including pain and grief. In the end, the Lord delivers His

The Holiness and Honor of Praise

own and will indeed subdue the enemies under our feet (Luke 10:19).

In Psalm 30:11 David praised God because He had girded him with *gladness*. The Hebrew word for "gladness" is *simchah,* which means "glee, blithesomeness, exceeding joy, or pleasure." Although we must endure sorrow in our lives from time to time, the Lord is faithful to bring us into the light of His joy.

The result of such growth is seen in Psalm 65. Here we find the *worship experience.* Verse 6 says it is *God who is girded with might.* He is a mighty God, and in Him we are secure. By resting in that fact, we can walk through pain and grief, knowing the Lord will lead us safely into His perfect joy.

The Breastpiece of Judgment

On the top of the ephod and over the heart was the breastpiece of judgment. This article, too, was made from gold with blue, purple, and scarlet material, and from fine twisted linen. The breastpiece was actually a square pouch, set with twelve precious and semi-precious stones. Each stone bore the name of one of the tribes of Israel, and it was attached to the ephod by blue and gold cords.

> And Aaron shall carry the names of the sons of Israel in the breastpiece of judgment over his heart when he enters the holy place, for a memorial before the Lord continually.
>
> Exodus 28:29

The breastpiece is a picture of our responsibility to intercede on behalf of God's people through prayer. It also reminds us that no single Christian is "an island unto himself," but each is an intricate part of the Body of Christ.

Inside the breastpiece were the Urim and Thummim, which literally means "light" and "perfection, or complete truth," respectively. As priests before God and man, we are to carry both the written Word, or *logos*, and the revealed Word, or *rhema*, close to our hearts. We are responsible to the Body to encourage, admonish, and exhort one another in love, according to Hebrews 3:13, Colossians 1:28, and 2 Timothy 4:2. We are instructed in Colossians 3:16, "Let the word of Christ richly dwell within you; with all wisdom teaching and admonishing one another with psalms and hymns and spiritual songs, singing with thankfulness in your hearts to God."

The Linen Turban

Wrapped around the priest's head was a fine linen mitre, or turban, reminding us that we are not to be conformed to this world but transformed by the renewing of our minds (Romans 12:2). First Corinthians 2:16 says that "we have the mind of Christ." The gospels indicate that Jesus' mind was totally submissive to the Father in all things. Philippians 2:5-8 says:

> Have this attitude in yourselves which was also in Christ Jesus, who, although He existed in the form of God, did not regard equality with God a thing to be grasped, but emptied Himself, taking the form of a bondservant, and being made in the likeness of men. And being found in appearance as a man, He humbled

The Holiness and Honor of Praise

Himself by becoming obedient to the point of death, even death on a cross.

Jesus did not have to prove himself; He was secure in knowing who He was. Because of this, He was able to humble himself as as servant. When we begin to recognize fully who we are in Christ, that is, sons and joint-heirs with Him, we will be able to live humbly as servants to men and woman in God's name.

The Gold Crown

Fastened to the turban by a blue cord was a beautiful gold plate, or crown, with the words, "Holy to the Lord," inscribed on it. This crown declares that we have put on salvation and been filled with the Holy Spirit, that we are walking in righteousness, reflecting His character, that we have been girded with truth and carry within us His light and life, and that we have let the mind of Christ dwell within us. This is a crown of *endurance*, yet even the Christian who is only beginning his walk with the Lord may wear it, for it is a sign of one's *willingness* to accept the work of God in his life. Thus, the gold crown of holiness allows us to enter the presence of the Lord.

> Pursue peace with all men, and the sanctification without which no one will see the Lord.
>
> Hebrews 12:14

Because Jesus was willing to wear the crown of thorns, we have the privilege of wearing some very important crowns:

Entering Into Worship: The Priest

The crown of glory and majesty (Psalm 8:5)
The crown of lovingkindness and compassion (Psalm 103:4)
The crown of knowledge (Proverbs 14:18)
The crown of righteousness (2 Timothy 4:8)
The crown of life (James 1:12)

Chapter 9
Anointed For Worship: The Oil

Before the priest could minister he had to be consecrated, or set apart, for the Lord's work. Leviticus 8 explains the procedure Aaron and his sons had to follow before they could carry out their duties in the Tabernacle.

First; they had to be washed with water and clothed with the priestly garments. Then the Tabernacle had to be anointed with oil, after which they themselves were anointed, the oil being poured over their heads. They offered several sacrifices, including a ram for ordination, which represented strength consecrated to God. The blood from that sacrifice was applied to the priest's right ear lobe, his right thumb, and the big toe of his right foot, signifying holiness in what he would hear, what he would do, and where he would go. Finally, the priests and their garments were sprinkled with blood and oil, followed by their sharing a meal. For seven days the priests spiritually prepared themselves within the Tabernacle, and only after that they were ready to go and minister on behalf of the people.

The Holiness and Honor of Praise

This is a picture of the spiritual preparation each of us must experience before we can minister to others in the name of the Lord. Moses, for example, was in the wilderness of Midian forty years before his mission in life was revealed to him (Acts 7:29-30). Paul spent three years after his conversion in the Arabian desert before he began his ministry (Galatians 1:17-18). Jesus himself spent forty days and forty nights in the wilderness facing temptation (Mark 1:12-15) before He began His public ministry, and that was after thirty years of growing "in wisdom and stature, and in favor with God and man" (Luke 2:52).

We too must be set apart for the work God has called us to do. We must allow the Word to wash us thoroughly as we are covered with the righteousness of Jesus. We must be filled with the Holy Spirit and accept the strength He gives us. We must learn to discern what He would have us hear, do, and where He would have us go. When we are identified with Christ in this way, we become partakers of His suffering; we learn what it means to hurt as He did, to know rejection, and to pay the cost so someone could be reconciled to God. Only then will our efforts to minister in the name of Jesus be effective. In Luke 10:33-34, for example, the Good Samaritan saw a wounded man and stopped to help. He anointed him with wine and oil and provided for his complete care. He demonstrated real compassion, which allowed the ailing man to recover. That is our call as well: to help those who are sick with sin, to bind their wounds with Christ's blood and the Holy Spirit, to love and care for them so they can find life and wholeness in Jesus.

The time we need to learn these things and prepare for the work to which God has called us varies from

Anointed For Worship: The Oil

individual to individual. Some learn God's lessons more quickly than others. Some need to take a great deal of time to be with the Lord just to find out who He really is, what His character and nature are like, and what His voice sounds like. Like the priests in the Tabernacle, we must be anointed for service, and the holy oil God instructed them to use gives us a clear picture of what we need to experience so we can minister as Jesus did.

1. Flowing Myrrh

The Hebrew word, *mowr*, means "grief, bitter."

> Blessed are those who mourn, for they shall be comforted. . . . Blessed are you when men revile you, and persecute you, and say all kinds of evil against you falsely, on account of Me. Rejoice, and be glad, for your reward in heaven is great, for so they persecuted the prophets who were before you.
>
> Matthew 5:4, 11-12

> Blessed be the God and Father of our Lord Jesus Christ, the Father of mercies and God of all comfort; who comforts us in all our affliction so that we may be able to comfort those who are in any affliction with the comfort with which we ourselves are comforted by God. For just as the sufferings of Christ are ours in abundance, so also our comfort is abundant through Christ.
>
> 2 Corinthians 1:3-5

The Greek word for suffering is *pathema* and means "hardship or pain." The root is *pathos*, which

The Holiness and Honor of Praise

means "passion, or affection for." There is a great deal of pain in the world today, but the suffering God has called us to prepare us for service as we come to know His heartbeat. This does not mean we simply bear up under destructive forces in our lives; we are called to be overcomers (Romans 8:37). As we walk in this authority and freedom, we will see more clearly the devastating effect sin has on a person. "Suffering for Jesus' sake," then, really means to be driven to pay the cost that would ultimately lead someone to restoration. The sorrow Jesus experienced in this life consisted of grief over rejection (Matthew 23:37) and the failure of His own to understand the life He was offering them (Matthew 17:17). Unless we have known such grief, we are unprepared to touch God and the hurting masses all around us. Yet, as we learn to bear one another's burdens, we too will undoubtedly come to appreciate the pain Jesus felt.

2. Fragrant Cinnamon

The Hebrew word, *qinnamown*, means "upright."

> The sacrifice of the wicked is an abomination to the Lord, but the prayer of the upright is His delight. The way of the wicked is an abomination to the Lord, but He loves him who pursues righteousness.
>
> Proverbs 15:8-9

> He made Him who knew no sin to be sin on our behalf, that we might become the righteousness of God in Him.
>
> 2 Corinthians 5:21

Anointed For Worship: The Oil

The only kind of uprightness, or righteousness, that pleases God is His own. Ours is at best "filthy rags" (Isaiah 64:6). But when we walk in His righteousness, we will be equipped to minister with a pure heart before the Lord. It is important to understand that righteousness is first of all imputed, as 2 Corinthians 5:21 tells us. But righteousness is also imparted to us daily as we make choices that please God. This is not always easy, since it means we may have to choose against what would naturally gratify the flesh. But the result of righteousness in our lives is a deep satisfaction of knowing we have honored the Lord, coupled with an assurance that we are stronger for having made the right choices.

3. Cane or Calamus

The Hebrew word, *qaneh*, means "an erect reed that resembles the rod, balanced in everything."

> O Lord, who may abide in Thy tent? Who may dwell on Thy holy hill? He who walks with integrity, and works righteousness, and speaks truth in his heart. He does not slander with his tongue, nor does evil to his neighbor, nor takes up a reproach against his friend; in whose eyes a reprobate is despised, but who honors those who fear the Lord; he swears to his own own hurt, and does not change; he does not put out his money at interest, nor does he take a bribe against the innocent. He who does these things will never be shaken.
>
> Psalm 15

The Holiness and Honor of Praise

> Therefore be imitators of God, as beloved children; and walk in love, just as Christ also loved you, and gave Himself up for us, an offering and a sacrifice to God as a fragrant aroma.
>
> Ephesians 5:1-2

> Be diligent to present yourself approved to God as a workman who does not need to be ashamed, handling accurately the word of truth.
>
> 2 Timothy 2:15

Balance for the Christian means a walk that reflects Jesus in every area. We must strive for personal integrity and learn to handle the Word of God with accuracy, always applying its content to our own lives first. The Hebrew word for "integrity" is *tom*, which means "completeness, prosperity, or innocence." When we study the Word and act on it, our lives begin to take on a sense of wholeness. We learn what it means to be "shrewd as serpents and innocent as doves" (Matthew 10:16).

4. Cassia

The Hebrew word, *qiddah*, means "shriveled"; its root, *qadad*, means "to bow down, to bend the neck and body in respect and submission."

> He must increase, but I must decrease.
>
> John 3:30

> Humble yourselves in the presence of the Lord, and He will exalt you.
>
> James 4:10

> For through the grace given to me I say to every man among you not to think more highly of himself than he ought to think; but to think so as to have sound judgment, as God has allotted to each a measure of faith.
>
> Romans 12:3

True submission is an attitude of the heart which desires to exalt the Lord in everything. Without humility it is impossible to see God, for as James 4:6 says, "God is opposed to the proud, but gives grace to the humble." Humility does not mean we continually put ourselves down, but rather we see ourselves clearly in the light of the Word. In doing so, we recognize not only the forgiveness we have in Christ but the calling and anointing which allows us to serve one another in His name.

5. Olive Oil

The Hebrew word, *zayith*, means "illuminating brightness"; *shemen* means "rich, fruitful."

> With the kind Thou dost show Thyself kind; with the blameless Thou dost show Thyself blameless; with the pure Thou dost show Thyself pure; and with the crooked Thou dost show Thyself astute. For Thou dost save an afflicted people; but haughty eyes Thou dost abase. For Thou dost light my lamp; the Lord my God illumines my darkness. For by Thee I can run upon a troop; and by my God I can leap over a wall.
>
> Psalm 18:25-29

The Holiness and Honor of Praise

> The Lord is my light and my salvation; whom shall I fear? The Lord is the defense of my life; whom shall I dread?
>
> Psalm 27:1

> Arise, shine; for your light has come, and the glory of the Lord has risen upon you. For behold, darkness will cover the earth, and deep darkness the peoples; but the Lord will rise upon you, and His glory will appear upon you. And nations will come to your light, and kings to the brightness of your rising.
>
> Isaiah 60:1-3

Just as all the other ingredients were dry until they were mixed with olive oil, it is the oil of the Holy Spirit which takes our grief, our upright walk, the balance and humility we demonstrate, and makes it all fruitful. Without the infilling of the Holy Spirit, the other elements lack power. As we walk in the light of Jesus and submit to His guidance, our ministry to people around us will produce *eternal* fruit for His glory.

> Behold, how good and how pleasant it is for brothers to dwell together in unity! It is like the precious oil upon the head, coming down upon the beard, even Aaron's beard, coming down upon the edge of his robes. It is like the dew of Hermon, coming down upon the mountains of Zion; for there the Lord commanded the blessing—life forever.
>
> Psalm 133

Chapter 10
The Individual Life of Praise

Dry ground is still visible in the Church today, and many people live in tremendous spiritual bondage. Distress, confusion, and heaviness are strongholds within the traditional Church at one extreme. A false sense of prosperity and strength have blinded the eyes of those intoxicated by pride. And because many have focused their attention on the gifts of the Spirit rather than the Giver, competition has resulted within religious circles at the other extreme. Whether in traditional or non-traditional churches, the ground is still very dry, and little fruit is being produced for God's kingdom.

In spite of everything, however, the Lord is coming for a spotless Bride. Out of the spiritual barrenness of our day, He is calling forth a people who will once again reflect His life in the world. As He prepared His chosen people two thousand years ago to receive His Son, He is now perfecting a Bride for the King of Glory—and that Bride will come from a holy people of praise.

The Holiness and Honor of Praise

Saints the world over are beginning to understand more clearly the nature and character of God. In the midst of a powerless Church He is searching for those who dare to believe, praise and worship Him simply for who He is, not just for what He can do for them. Mighty Jehovah has given us, His Church, the fullest revelation of himself through His *logos,* Jesus. Now He is calling those who will once again walk in complete obedience to His Word.

Many Christians today are seeking new depth to their walk, and corporately they desire to become a praising Church. But it is not possible to praise and worship God collectively unless this is a way of life privately. We cannot walk in freedom and authority as a Body if we do not experience freedom and authority individually. For this reason, the relationship we possess with the Father is of utmost importance. It *must* be nurtured, and it *must* be appreciated as the most precious treasure we could ever have.

It should be our greatest desire to live in the presence of God the Father; that is, after all, His greatest desire for us. As He invited the children of Israel to worship Him in the Tabernacle He designed in the wilderness, He challenges us to come into the Holy of Holies once again. We can only enter through the narrow gate as Luke 13:23-24 and Matthew 7:13-14 point out. We must be justified at the cross (Romans 6:3-4), washed by the water of the Word (Ephesians 5:25-27), and become partakers of His light (John 8:12). At His table of communion we find healing, strength, and the revelation of who He is (John 6:47-51). Thus, our life becomes one of prayer and praise as we nourish ourselves

The Individual Life of Praise

in Him (Psalm 141:2). It is at this point of praise that we are ushered into His presence where we behold Him in all His glory, and it is there we are forever changed.

Chapter 11
Worshiping in Spirit and Truth

The human spirit alone is incapable of praising God; at best praise would be heaped on itself for its own accomplishments. Praise for the Father originates in a spirit controlled by His Holy Spirit. This is why most Christians are not people of praise; they simply do not experience daily the fullness of God's Spirit.

One day Jesus appeared in His resurrected state to the disciples, He breathed on them and said, "Receive the Holy Spirit" (John 20:22). The Greek word for "breathed" is *emphusao* and means "to rest in or on." It comes from a root, denoting "the origin, or point where motion proceeds, ending in completion." In other words, Jesus took the deepest part of himself and planted it in the deepest part of His disciples. Furthermore, the word translated "receive" is *lambano* and means "accept and get hold of right now."

He then gave the disciples instructions to wait in Jerusalem "for what the Father had promised, 'Which,'

The Holiness and Honor of Praise

He said, 'you heard of from Me; for John baptized with water, but you shall be baptized with the Holy Spirit not many days from now' " (Acts 1:4-5).

Ten days later, on the Day of Pentecost, the disciples were empowered by the Spirit of God. Had they not been sealed with the Spirit already, they could not have waited in an upper room for fifty days without knowing what they were waiting for. But in obedience to the Spirit who indwelt them, they did wait—and God poured out His anointing power beyond anything the world had ever seen since the day He breathed into Adam His breath of Life.

In the Garden of Eden God had breathed His life, courage, spirit and mind into man and made him a living soul, equipped with all the authority and freedom he would need to rule over God's creation. On the day of His resurrection Jesus again breathed into man and restored the authority and freedom man had given to Satan. It was on the Day of Pentecost, however, that the disciples were overwhelmed with God's life-changing, world-changing power, ushered in "like a violent, rushing wind" (Acts 2:2).

Throughout the New Testament, believers were empowered by the Holy Spirit in one of four ways. Some received power at the moment they were saved (Acts 2:38). Some waited in obedience and prayer for God's power to fall on them (Acts 2:1-4). Others were filled simply by listening to the message of God (Acts 10:44). Still other received God's power through the laying on of hands (Acts 8:17; 19:6, and 2 Timothy 1:6).

Today the infilling and empowering by the Holy Spirit should be simultaneous, but too often it isn't, primarily because we do not realize what God has preordained for us. Still, the promise of the Father remains the same.

> And I say to you, ask, and it shall be given to you; seek, and you shall find; knock, and it shall be opened. For everyone who asks, receives; and he who seeks, finds; and to him who knocks, it shall be opened. Now suppose one of you fathers is asked by his son for a fish; he will not give him a snake instead of a fish, will he? Or if he is asked for an egg, he will not give him a scorpion, will he? If you then, being evil, know how to give good gifts to your children, how much more shall your Heavenly Father give the Holy Spirit to those who ask Him?
>
> Luke 11:9-13

It is God's will for all His children to be filled with His Spirit.

> And do not get drunk with wine, for that is dissipation, but be filled with the Spirit, speaking to one another in psalms and hymns and spiritual songs, singing and making melody with your heart to the Lord; always giving thanks for all things in the name of our Lord Jesus Christ to God, even the Father; and be subject to one another in the fear of Christ.
>
> Ephesians 5:18-21

On the Day of Pentecost bystanders wondered if the disciples were drunk with wine when, in fact, they were

The Holiness and Honor of Praise

filled with the Holy Spirit. It is His Spirit which produces true joy and lasting security.

To be filled with the Spirit means we seek after the Lord with our total being. It means we desire to live in His presence. It means we recognize ourselves as vessels of holy praise, bringing glory and honor to God alone.

To be filled with the Spirit means we have let go of the flesh so God could *pleroos* us, or "make us replete, to cram us full of himself, to level up our hollows, to furnish and satisfy us, and to finish us." The root word, *pletho*, means "to fulfill and accomplish," reflecting God's nature and work on our behalf.

Whenever people were filled with the Spirit in the Scriptures, there were changes in their lives. Today many people assume that the evidence of a Spirit-filled life is the manifestation of tongues; but is it? In almost every incident where the Holy Spirit came upon His people, speaking in tongues or prophesying did occur, but to make a blanket statement declaring that speaking in tongues is the primary or only evidence is to go a step beyond the written Word of God.

> But to each one is given the manifestation of
> the Spirit for the common good.
> 1 Corinthians 12:7

With the infilling of the Spirit comes an obvious difference. Jesus said, '. . . you shall receive power when the Holy Spirit has come upon you; and you shall be My witnesses . . ." (Acts 1:8). We can say unequivocally that *power* is *the* evidence we have.

The gift of tongues as found in 1 Corinthians 12 is to be accompanied with an interpretation, because the gifts are

Worshiping in Spirit and Truth

given to edify the assembled Body; and, without an interpreter, our minds are unfruitful. In 1 Corinthians 14, however, we find that tongues edify the individual as well because he is speaking to God, spirit to Spirit.

Instructions are given to those who exercise the gift of tongues within as assembly of believers;

> So also you, since you are zealous for spiritual gifts, seek to abound for the edification of the church. Therefore let one who speaks in a tongue pray that he may interpret.
> 1 Corinthians 14:12-13

Likewise, there are instructions for those who do not speak in tongues:

> Therefore, my brethren, desire earnestly to prophesy, and do not forbid to speak in tongues. But let all things be done properly and in an orderly manner.
> 1 Corinthians 14:39-40

> Now I wish that you all spoke in tongues. . . .
> 1 Corinthians 14:5

Without fail those who were filled with the Spirit of God were changed, and their lives reflected His Word and work. Philip, for example, was moved by the Spirit to witness to the Ethiopian (Acts 8:26-40). Stephen, full of the Holy Ghost, looked directly into glory while he was being stoned to death (Acts 7:55-56). Priscilla and Aquila opened up their home for ministry because they were filled with the Spirit, and yet left their home to travel with Paul and teach the Word (Acts 18:2-3, 18-19, 25-26). Barnabas was able to encourage the Christians in Antioch

The Holiness and Honor of Praise

"to remain true to the Lord; for he was a good man, and full of the Holy Spirit and of faith. And considerable numbers were brought to the Lord" (Acts 11:19-24).

In every situation the people who were filled with the Spirit were equipped with whatever they needed to minister effectively. They were given the motivational gift, ministry gift or manifestation gift appropriate to the moment (1 Corinthians 12:4-7). The timing and suitability was determined not by the individual, but by the Spirit himself.

> But one and the same Spirit works all these things, distributing to each one individually just as He wills.
>
> 1 Corinthians 12:11

The *motivational gifts* are listed in Romans 12:6-8. The Greek word to describe this category is *energema*, meaning "an effect, operation, a working." Its root, *energeo*, means "to be active and efficient," and this word comes from *en*, meaning "position," and *ergon*, meaning "work or labor." We get our English word "energy" from these roots. In other words, these gifts put us in a position to be efficient because they are inspiring for us personally. The gifts included here are:

> **Prophecy** (Greek, *propheteia*): "a prophecy or prediction"; its root, *prophetes*, means "an inspired speaker, a foreteller."
>
> **Serving** (Greek, *diakonia*): "attendance, aid, service, minister, relief."
>
> **Teaching** (Greek, *didasko*): "to teach"; form of a primitive verb, meaning "to learn."

Worshiping in Spirit and Truth

Exhortation (Greek, *paraklesis*): "imploration, solace, comfort, consolation, exhortation" (Jesus said He would send another Comforter, the Holy Spirit, who is the *parakletos*, "the intercessor, consoler, advocate, comforter").

Giving (Greek, *metadidomi*): "to give over, to share."

Leadership (Greek, *proistemi*): "to stand before, to preside, to maintain, be over, rule."

Mercy (Greek, *eleeo*): "compassionate by word or deed, by divine grace."

The *ministry gifts* are found in Ephesians 4:11-12 and in part of 1 Corinthians 12:27-28. The Greek word for "ministry" is *diakonia*, meaning "attendance, service, minister, office, relief." Its root is *diako*, which means "waiter, teacher, pastor, deacon, deaconess, servant." These gifts are to be used "for the equipping of the saints for the work of service, to the building up of the body of Christ; until we all attain to the unity of the faith, and the knowledge of the Son of God, to a mature man, to the measure of the stature which belongs to the fulness of Christ" (Ephesians 4:12-13). The ministry gifts include:

Apostles (Greek, *apostolos*): "a delegate, an ambassador of the gospel, a commissioner of Christ, a messenger." Its root *apostello*, means "set apart and sent out."

Prophets (Greek, *prophetes*): "a foreteller, an inspired speaker, a prophet."

The Holiness and Honor of Praise

Evangelists (Greek, *euaggelistes*): "a preacher of the gospel." Its root, *euaggelizo*, means "to announce good news, to declare and preach."

Pastors (Greek, *poimen*): "shepherd, pastor."

Teachers (Greek, *didaskalos*): "an instructor."

The *manifestation gifts* are found in 1 Corinthians 12:8-10. The Greek word for "manifestation" is *phanerosis*, meaning "exhibition, expression." Its root, *phaneroo*, means "to render apparent," and the root for that word is *phaneros*, "to shine publically." These gifts are the effect of the motivational gifts and ministry gifts being put into action. They include:

Word of Wisdom (Greek, *logo, sophia*): "the divine expression of earthly or spiritual wisdom, clear and wise."

Word of Knowledge (Greek, *logo, gnosis*): "the divine expression of knowing, being aware of, perceiving, being sure of, understanding."

Faith (Greek, *pistis*): "persuasion, conviction of religious truth, especially one's reliance on God, constancy in profession, assurance, belief, faith, fidelity."

Healing (Greek, *iama*): "a cure." Its root, *iaomai*, means "to heal, make whole."

Miracles (Greek, *dunamis*): "miraculous power, ability, abundance, mighty in deed, strength." Its root *dunamai*, means "to be able, possible, to be of power."

Worshiping in Spirit and Truth

Prophecy (Greek, *propheteuo*): "to foretell events, divine, speak under inspiration, exercise the prophetic office."

Discerning of Spirits (Greek, *diakrisis, pneuma*): "judicial estimation of breath (life), rational soul, angel, demon, divine God."

Tongues (Greek, *glossa*): "language not naturally acquired."

Interpretation (Greek, *hermeneia*): "translation."

There is nothing in Scripture that says we receive only one gift from the Spirit. In fact, the more Jesus is at home in us the more we should move as He moved, displaying any or all of the gifts appropriate to the circumstances.

It is an absolute necessity for any believer desiring an overwhelming life of praise to be filled with the Holy Spirit. A person who is full of self or religion simply cannot experience God's fullness at the same time. Although every Christian has the indwelling presence of God, it is only the one who is so possessed by Him whose life becomes a river of praise. Yet this is a decision which involves choice, need, surrender, asking for and receiving all that God has for us.

Chapter 12
The Unity of the Faith: Worshiping With Other Believers

And they were continually devoting themselves to the apostles' teaching and to fellowship, to the breaking of bread and to prayer. And everyone kept feeling a sense of awe; and many wonders and signs were taking place through the apostles. And all those who had believed were together, and had all things in common; and they began selling their property and possessions, and were sharing them with all, as anyone might have need. And day by day continuing with one mind in the temple, and breaking bread from house to house, they were taking their meals together with gladness and sincerity of heart, praising God, and having favor with all the people. And the Lord was adding to their number day by day those who were being saved.

Acts 2:42-47

The Holiness and Honor of Praise

The first-century church was a praising church because of the reality of God in their midst. They were a people who knew what it meant to have a "broken and contrite heart" (Psalm 51:17), and out of gratitude their praise for the Lord flowed. Probably the best example of this is Mary Magdalene. Set free from seven demons, she devoted her life to following Jesus and ministering to Him (Luke 8:1-3). She was willing to stand at the foot of the cross with Jesus' mother and His mother's sister when nearly everyone else had deserted Him (Matthew 27:56). Mary Magdalene remained faithful to the end, and as a result, Jesus appeared to her first after His resurrection (Mark 16:9).

> For this reason I say to you, her sins, which are many, have been forgiven, for she loved much, but he who is forgiven little, loves little.
> Luke 7:47

It is not possible for us to enter the presence of Holy God without a repentant heart, being full of appreciation for who He is and what He has done for us.

Worship is far more than coming together for three hymns, an offering, the special music, a sermon, and an altar call. The presumption that we have entered into true worship without first humbling ourselves before the Lord is totally unscriptural.

> Humble yourselves in the presence of the Lord, and He will exalt you.
> James 4:10

Worship is an intimate act. The Greek word is *proskuneo*, meaning "to kiss, reverence, bow down before,

The Unity of the Faith: Worshiping With Other Believers

---

to become prostrate." Unfortunately, in most churches today, we talk about God but rarely talk to Him or exalt Him. We often try to "schedule" His appearance on Sundays, Wednesdays or during the week for a special "revival," and expect Him to act as we have been doctrinally trained. For many Christians, the thought of letting God be who He is and was in the New Testament is frightening, and yet *He cannot, and will not be less than who He says He is.* How sad it must make God to see how far away the Church has moved from the one He established through the power of His Son. Even though the ground is very dry in the Church, the call rings clearly:

> Sow with a view to righteousness, reap in accordance with kindness; break up your fallow ground, for it is time to seek the Lord until He comes to rain righteousness on you.
>
> Hosea 10:12

> For I will pour out water on the thirsty land and streams on the dry ground; I will pour out My Spirit on your offspring, and My blessing on your descendants; and they will spring up among the grass like poplars by streams of water.
>
> Isaiah 44:3-4

The Purpose of the Church

According to the Scriptures, the purpose God laid out for the Church is threefold:

 1. To minister to Him
 2. To minister to the needs of the Body
 3. To evangelize the world

The Holiness and Honor of Praise

More often than not, we put emphasis on evangelization first, but God puts the emphasis on "continuing with one mind" and being devoted "to the apostles' teaching and to fellowship, to the breaking of bread and to prayer." With awesome respect for God, we open ourselves to Him and to one another, and *He* adds to our number day by day those who are being saved (see Acts 2:42-47).

It seems easier to approach another person with the gospel than to come into the presence of God, but the result of such effort may not be as fruitful as we imagine. When we go witnessing for the sake of "doing our spiritual duty" without first coming to an understanding of God's holiness through experience, our witness of Him lacks power.

However, if we witness in the anointed power of the Holy Spirit for the glory of God, the Spirit has opportunity to bear fruit in the lives of those to whom we are talking.

> Not that we are adequate in ourselves to consider anything as coming from ourselves, but our adequacy is from God, who also made us adequate as servants of a new covenant, not of the letter, but of the Spirit; for the letter kills, but the Spirit gives life.
>
> 2 Corinthians 3:5-6

God's plan from the beginning was to establish a fruitful relationship with man. Jesus came to reconcile us with the Father, and it is He who leads us into His presence in worship. We minister to Him through our praise; this is the only thing we can offer to God because it is the offering of ourselves.

The Unity of the Faith: Worshiping With Other Believers

Whoever stands as the praise leader, whether pastor, music director, or another, must first humble himself in the presence of the Lord. This is vital if the praise leader is to bring the people from praise to true worship, which is a very individual act. We might come together to praise God collectively, but at the recognition of His glory, every heart must bow down. If we share the unity of our minds, we will know when God has come on the scene. But it is the leader's responsibility to usher the people in with instructions concerning a humble attitude and to encourage their exaltation of Almighty God.

> Come, let us worship and bow down; let us kneel before the Lord our Maker. For He is our God, and we are the people of His pasture, and the sheep of His hand.
>
> Psalm 95:6-7a

Am I My Brother's Keeper?

> Now therefore arise, cross this Jordan, you and all this people, to the land which I am giving to them, to the sons of Israel. Every place on which the sole of your foot treads, I have given it to you, just as I spoke to Moses. From the wilderness and . . . as far as . . . the river Euphrates, all the Land of the Hittites, and as far as the Great Sea toward the setting of the sun, will be your territory. No man will be able to stand before you all the days of your life. Just as I have been with Moses, I will be with you; I will not fail you or forsake you. Be strong and courageous, for you shall give this people

The Holiness and Honor of Praise

> possession of the land which I swore to their fathers to give them. Only be strong and very courageous; be careful to do according to all the law which Moses My servant commanded you; do not turn from it to the right or to the left, so that you may have success wherever you go. This book of the law shall not depart from your mouth, but you shall meditate on it day and night, so that you may be careful to do according to all that is written in it; for then you will make your way prosperous, and then you will have success. Have I not commanded you? Be strong and courageous! Do not tremble or be dismayed, for the Lord your God is with you wherever you go.
>
> Joshua 1:2-9

When looking at the children of Israel and their journey toward the Promised Land, we can see ourselves and the journey we are making toward the fullest life possible in Jesus.

> I gave you a land on which you had not labored, and cities which you had not built, and you have lived in them; you are eating of vineyards and oliveyards which you did not plant.
>
> Joshua 24:13

> For this reason I say to you, do not be anxious for your life, as to what you shall eat, or what you shall drink; nor for your body, as to what you shall put on. Is not life more than food, and the body than clothing? Look at the

The Unity of the Faith: Worshiping With Other Believers

> birds of the air, that they do not sow, neither do they reap, nor gather into barns, and yet your heavenly Father feeds them. Are you not worth much more than they? . . . But seek first His kingdom and His righteousness; and all these things shall be added to you.
>
> Matthew 6:25-26, 33

The story of Israel is a picture of our spiritual pilgrimage. Moses is a type for Jesus, leading us out of Egypt, or sin, through the Red Sea into new birth and into the wilderness, where we learn to trust God for provisions, authority and direction. The wilderness experience was not meant to last forty years, but God was willing to take as much time as necessary to teach His people what they needed to know: obedience. It was only their sin that kept them from entering the Promised Land much earlier.

Before Moses died he promised the people Joshua would lead them into Canaan. Likewise, before Jesus ascended into heaven He promised He would send One like himself to "guide you into all the truth; for He will not speak on His own initiative, but whatever He hears, He will speak; and He will disclose to you what is to come. He shall glorify Me; for He shall take of Mine, and shall disclose it to you" (John 16:13-14).

Joshua is a type for the Holy Spirit, who desires to take God's people across the Jordan where they die to self and into Canaan where they find abundant life.

There are many Christians who have come out of Egypt but never make it out of the wilderness. They live and die never knowing the joy of emptying oneself and being filled with the life of God.

The Holiness and Honor of Praise

But for those who choose to enter in, God requires their total submission and obedience. He knows that in order to find true freedom, there will be many battles to fight, which must be fought in His strength alone. That is why God told His people in Joshua 1 to be strong and courageous. Alliances with the world have always been forbidden by God, because they lead people into deception.

God's people are to be separate, because the world will never offer to meet our needs without expecting something in return. Sometimes what is expected is control of our thoughts and opinions, but we can be sure that the day will come when we must pay.

Christians cannot find pure and lasting solutions outside of Christ and His Body, because we have a new nature created to respond to the promptings of the Holy Spirit. Once we recognize this we can begin to appreciate the role we have in each other's lives.

Ministry takes on many forms: physical, emotional and spiritual. In light of spiritual ministry to our brothers and sisters in the faith, it is important that our motives be right. It is very difficult to help someone who has a speck of impurity in his eye when a log is lodged in our own (Matthew 7:3-5).

> Brethren, even if a man is caught in any trespass, you who are spiritual, restore such a one in a spirit of gentleness; looking to yourself, lest you too be tempted.
>
> Galatians 6:1

When we begin to minister to each other in a spirit of humility rather than judgment, we will reflect God's

The Unity of the Faith: Worshiping With Other Believers

---

unconditional love. Our hearts will then be filled with praise for Him, because we can see His work not only in the lives of our brothers and sisters but in our own as well.

> So then, while we have opportunity, let us do good to all men, and especially to those who are of the household of the faith.
>
> Galatians 6:10

Out of a heart full of praise to God comes a life of service, both to the Body of Christ and to the lost in order to lead them to the light. The Church is given several specific responsibilities in the Scriptures, and today they are needed more than ever. Jesus set the example for us, and as His Body we are to minister exactly as He did.

Meeting Spiritual Needs Through:

Encouragement (1 Thessalonians 5:11)

Teaching (Colossians 1:28 and 3:16)

Prayer (1 Thessalonians 5:12, 17)

Admonition (Colossians 3:16 and 1 Thessalonians 5:14)

Correction (2 Timothy 2:25)

Meeting Physical Needs Through:

Feeding the Hungry (Matthew 25:35)

Giving to the Poor (Deuteronomy 15:7-11 and 1 Timothy 6:17-19)

Sharing with the Needy (Acts 2:44-45 and James 2:1-18)

Visiting the Widows and Orphans (1 Timothy 5:3-10, 16)

Visiting Those in Jail (Matthew 25:35-40)

The Holiness and Honor of Praise

Praying for the Sick (James 5:14-18)

Giving to the Ministry (Philippians 4:16-19)

Showing Hospitality to Strangers (Hebrews 13:2 and Romans 12:13)

Meeting Emotional Needs Through:
Encouragement (Philippians 2:1-2)

Counsel (Proverbs 13:10 and 19:2-21)

Listening (James 1:19-20)

Comfort (1 Thessalonians 4:13-18)

It is interesting to note the similarities between our response to those in need spiritually and those in need emotionally. The primary difference is that with those who are suffering emotionally we are to listen and offer comfort and godly counsel. With those who are in error spiritually there may be times when we are called upon to admonish and correct, but always in a spirit of gentleness (Galatians 6:1).

Whether we have ministered spiritually, physically or emotionally, every "cup of cold water" given to one of His little ones shall not go unrewarded (Matthew 10:42).

> For just as we have many members in one body and all the members do not have the same function, so we, who are many, are one body in Christ, and individually members of one another. . . . Let love be without hypocrisy. Abhor what is evil; cling to what is good. Be devoted to one another in brotherly love; give preference to one another in honor; not lagging

The Unity of the Faith: Worshiping With Other Believers

behind in diligence, fervent in spirit, serving the Lord; rejoicing in hope, persevering in tribulation, devoted to prayer, contributing to the needs of the saints, practicing hospitality. Bless those who persecute you; bless and curse not. Rejoice with those who rejoice, and weep with those who weep. Be of the same mind toward one another; do not be haughty in mind, but associate with the lowly. Do not be wise in your own estimation. Never pay back evil for evil to anyone. Respect what is right in the sight of all men. If possible, so far as it depends on you, be at peace with all men. Never take your own revenge, beloved, but leave room for the wrath of God, for it is written, "Vengeance is Mine, I will repay, says the Lord." "But if your enemy is hungry, feed him, and if he is thirsty, give him a drink; for in so doing you will heap burning coals upon his head." Do not be overcome by evil, but overcome evil with good.

Romans 12:4-5, 9-21

"Lord, when did we see You hungry, and feed You, or thirsty and give You drink? And when did we see You a stranger, and invite You in, or naked, and clothe You? And when did we see You sick, or in prison, and come to You?" And the King will answer and say to them, "Truly I say to you, to the extent that you did it to one of these brothers of Mine, even the least of them, you did it to Me."

Matthew 25:36-40

Chapter 13
"You Shall Be My Witnesses": The Ministry of Reconciliation

As we have seen, the Church was established for three reasons:

1. To worship God and minister to Him;
2. To meet the needs of His Body; and
3. To be witnesses of His life within us.

We tend to think of "going witnessing," but the Greek translation for the word "witness" is *martus*, meaning "martyr." As Christians, we died to sin at the Cross and now have the privilege of living in God's presence each day.

> For if we have become united with Him in the likeness of His death, certainly we shall be also in the likeness of His resurrection, knowing this, that our old self was crucified with Him, that our body of sin might be done away with, that we should no longer be slaves

The Holiness and Honor of Praise

> to sin; for he who has died is freed from sin. Now if we have died with Christ, we believe that we shall also live with Him, knowing that Christ, having been raised from the dead, is never to die again; death no longer is master over Him. For the death that He died, He died to sin, once for all; but the life that He lives, He lives to God. Even so consider yourselves to be dead to sin, but alive to God in Christ Jesus.
>
> Romans 6:5-11

To be a witness is to be a first-hand observer of something that has happened. It is a personal account of the power and grace of Jesus in our lives. Its meaning never fades and because our relationship with God is a growing one, our witness is always fresh.

We are witnesses to the sanctification taking place in our lives. In other words, we know we are being purified in order to serve God in true holiness. We are witnesses of a great exchange, His righteousness for our corruption.

> For when you were slaves of sin, you were freed in regard to righteousness. Therefore what benefit were you then deriving from the things of which you are now ashamed? For the outcome of those things is death. But now having been freed from sin and enslaved to God, you derive your benefit, resulting in sanctification, and the outcome, eternal life.
>
> Romans 6:20-22

"You Shall Be My Witnesses"

The gospel is indeed good news. Ours is a message of hope, and only the Christian who recognizes that he has been freed from sin and is being conformed to the image of Christ will be the kind of witness Jesus commissioned us to be.

Salvation has always been a work of God's Spirit, and it is His wooing power alone which brings men to the realization of their sin and His righteousness. We may wish we could bring everyone we know to the saving knowledge of Jesus Christ, but only those who have been called first by God will be capable of responding to the gospel. Thus, it is no longer a matter of pressuring an individual into repeating the "sinner's prayer" but rather waiting on the Holy Spirit as He convicts a person of his sin at a time when he is able to receive the truth. As we grow in the Lord we will be more sensitive to His leading when we share the gospel.

If we go witnessing out of a need to fulfill a religious obligation, we run the risk of adding more tares to the church. Salvation comes only when there is true repentance for sin. An individual must experience godly sorrow and desire for God to change his life.

> For the sorrow that is according to the will of God produces a repentance without regret, leading to salvation; but the sorrow of the world produces death.
>
> 2 Corinthians 7:10

It is tragic that our churches are filled with people who have never experienced godly sorrow or a desire for holiness. Many are afraid of going to hell but have no personal revelation of who Jesus is.

The Holiness and Honor of Praise

The Lord will make himself irresistible to those seeking the truth, and it is our privilege to be the instrument through which He may reveal himself.

> Let your light shine before men in such a way that they may see your good works, and glorify your Father who is in heaven.
>
> Matthew 5:16

As we live in the light of His glory, we will speak His words confidently and the darkness will flee. Our bold faith in God will be evident only as we abide in His presence.

> Now as they observed the confidence of Peter and John, and understood that they were uneducated and untrained men, they were marveling, and began to recognize them as having been with Jesus.
>
> Acts 4:13

The Church has every opportunity today to be trained in the Scriptures. In fact, we are commanded to

> Be diligent to present yourself approved to God as a workman who does not need to be ashamed, handling accurately the word of truth.
>
> 2 Timothy 2:15

Peter and John not only walked with Jesus, but they waited for the anointing of His Spirit which came at Pentecost. It is the Holy Spirit in the life of a witness that makes Jesus irresistible. The fuller we are, the more evident He is.

"You Shall Be My Witnesses"

Possibly the greatest witness in the sense of *martureo*, meaning "to testify or bear record" was John the Baptist. Instead of being an eyewitness to the fulfillment of Jesus' mission, His death and resurrection, John announced the beginning of His ministry. John the Baptist was a voice "crying in the wilderness" (Luke 3:4), whom God used to prepare the people for the gift of salvation.

> He who comes after me has a higher rank than I, for He existed before me.
>
> John 1:15
>
> I am not the Christ, but I have been sent before Him.
>
> John 3:28
>
> As for me, I baptize you with water, but He who is mightier than I is coming, and I am not fit to untie the thong of His sandals; He Himself will baptize you in the Holy Spirit and fire. And His winnowing fork is in His hand to clean out His threshing floor, and to gather the wheat into His barn; but He will burn up the chaff with unquenchable fire.
>
> Luke 3:16-17

John the Baptist *bore witness* of the judgment of sin which was to come. John, the apostle, however, *was a witness* of the unconditional grace of God.

> What was from the beginning, what we have heard, what we have seen with our eyes, what we beheld and our hands handled, concerning the Word of life—and the life was manifested, and we have seen and bear witness and

The Holiness and Honor of Praise

> proclaim to you the eternal life, which was with the Father and was manifested to us—what we have seen and heard we proclaim to you also, that you also may have fellowship with us; and indeed our fellowship is with the Father, and with His Son Jesus Christ. And these things we write, so that our joy may be made complete.
>
> 1 John 1:1-4

John the Baptist played a distinct role in the history of the Church and was, in fact, martyred for his bold witness. But a better model for us is John, the beloved apostle, who leaned upon Jesus and ate from His holy hand. It is this intimacy, coupled with the Holy Spirit's empowering, which produces unshakable confidence. We are not obliged, then, "to witness" but *become* natural witnesses of what we have seen and heard and felt in our own lives.

> And we know that the Son of God has come, and has given us understanding, in order that we might know Him who is true, and we are in Him who is true, in His Son Jesus Christ. This is the true God and eternal life.
>
> 1 John 5:20

As witnesses, the greatest privilege we have is to proclaim liberty to the captives. For the lost person who is reaching out, it is our responsibility to point him to the Cross. For the Christian living in bondage to sin, we are charged to announce by the authority of God's Word that his sins have been forgiven. To the unrepentant sinner we must declare the severity of the Lord, that unless he turns from his ways to seek God, he will surely die.

> Behold then the kindness and severity of God; to those who fell, severity, but to you, God's kindness, if you continue in His kindness, otherwise, you also will be cut off. And they also, if they do not continue in their unbelief, will be grafted in; for God is able to graft them in again.
>
> Romans 11:22-23

This message of salvation is not a message of "pie in the sky by and by," but a wonderful announcement of *yeshuah*, "deliverance, health, help, welfare, victory, and prosperity." It is the declaration of *teshuah*, "the provision of safety" (Colossians 1:13-14). It is the fulfillment of God's Law, written upon our hearts. Jesus stands as our *soter*, (Greek, Savior), the defender of our faith.

Is it any wonder that such an exchange of sin for the very righteousness of God himself is called "good news"?

> Therefore if any man is in Christ, he is a new creature; the old things passed away; behold, new things have come.
>
> 2 Corinthians 5:17

This is the announcement of forgiveness we are to share with our world.

> Now all these things are from God, who reconciled us to Himself through Christ, and gave us the ministry of reconciliation, namely,

The Holiness and Honor of Praise

that God was in Christ reconciling the world to Himself, not counting their trespasses against them, and He has committed to us the word of reconciliation.

2 Corinthians 5:18-19

We are a people chosen of God to live and walk in holiness, to serve one another in love and to allow Jesus to make himself irresistible to a world dying in sin. We have a mighty and wonderful God, and it is such an honor to praise Him. We encourage you to seek Him with your whole heart, let Him fill you with His Spirit and bring you into His presence where you were meant to live.

I will extol Thee, my God, O King;
And I will bless Thy name forever and ever.
Every day I will bless Thee,
And I will praise Thy name forever and ever.
Great is the Lord, and highly to be praised;
And His greatness is unsearchable.
One generation shall praise Thy works to another,
And shall declare Thy mighty acts.
On the glorious splendor of Thy majesty,
And on Thy wonderful works, I will meditate
And men shall speak of the power of Thy awesome acts;
And I will tell of Thy greatness.
They shall eagerly utter the memory of Thine abundant goodness,
And shall shout joyfully of Thy righteousness.
The Lord is gracious and merciful;
Slow to anger and great in lovingkindness.
The Lord is good to all,

And His mercies are over all His works.
All Thy works shall give thanks to Thee, O Lord,
And Thy godly ones shall bless Thee.
They shall speak of the glory of Thy kingdom,
And talk of Thy power;
To make known to the sons of men Thy mighty acts,
And the glory of the majesty of Thy kingdom,
Thy Kingdom is an everlasting Kingdom,
And Thy dominion endures throughout all generations.
The Lord sustains all who fall,
And raises up all who are bowed down.
The eyes of all look to Thee,
And Thou dost give them their food in due time.
Thou dost open Thy hand,
And dost satisfy the desire of every living thing.
The Lord is righteous in all His ways.
And kind in all His deeds,
The Lord is near to all who call upon Him,
To all who call upon Him in truth.
He will fulfill the desire of those who fear Him;
He will also hear their cry and will save them.
The Lord keeps all who love Him;
But all the wicked, He will destroy.
My mouth will speak the praise of the Lord;
And all flesh will bless His holy name forever and ever.

Psalm 145